名师名校名校长

凝聚名师共识
回应名师关怀
打造名师品牌
培育名师群体

名师名校名校长书系

玩转英语课堂的微视频
——初中英语课堂微视频的设计与实施

曾素文 / 主编

吉林人民出版社

图书在版编目（CIP）数据

玩转英语课堂的微视频：初中英语课堂微视频的设计与实施 / 曾素文主编. — 长春：吉林人民出版社，2019.9

ISBN 978-7-206-16403-3

Ⅰ.①玩… Ⅱ.①曾… Ⅲ.①英语课－课堂教学－教学研究－初中 Ⅳ.①G633.412

中国版本图书馆CIP数据核字（2019）第216412号

玩转英语课堂的微视频——初中英语课堂微视频的设计与实施
WANZHUAN YINGYU KETANG DE WEISHIPIN——CHUZHONG YINGYU KETANG WEISHIPIN DE SHEJI YU SHISHI

主　　编：曾素文	封面设计：姜　龙

责任编辑：张　娜
助理编辑：赵元元
吉林人民出版社出版发行（长春市人民大街7548号　邮政编码：130022）
印　　刷：北京虎彩文化传播有限公司
开　　本：787mm×1092mm　1/16
印　　张：12　　　　　　字　　数：216千字
标准书号：ISBN 978-7-206-16403-3
版　　次：2022年6月第1版　印　　次：2022年6月第1次印刷
定　　价：45.00元

如发现印装质量问题，影响阅读，请与出版社联系调换。

编 委 会

主　编：曾素文

编　委：（排名不分前后）

庄秋蚕　郑艳霞　李雪娟　罗育梅

目录

第一章

"微课"在英语教学中的应用 …… 1

"微课"在初中英语课堂教学中的应用初探 …… 2
"微课"在初中英语课堂教学中的应用优势 …… 8

第二章

听力技能的微视频设计与实施 …… 13

初中英语课堂听力技能微视频实施的必要性 …… 14
初中英语课堂听力技能微视频实施的可行性 …… 16
初中英语课堂听力技能微视频实施的教学案例 …… 19
初中英语课堂听力技能微视频实施的问题和对策 …… 24

第三章

阅读技能的微视频设计与实施 …… 41

基于阅读学情的初中英语微视频设计 …… 42
初中英语阅读微视频教学的具体实施 …… 55

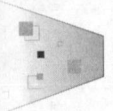

第四章
专题语法的微视频设计与实施 ·············· 73

语法微视频教学的技巧 ·············· 74
初中语法微视频教学的具体实施 ·············· 81

第五章
话题写作的微视频设计与实施 ·············· 99

话题式微课教学的设计 ·············· 100
初中话题写作微视频教学课例 ·············· 112

第六章
文化意识的微视频设计与实施 ·············· 141

有关文化意识培养的作文微视频教学设计 ·············· 142
初中文化意识培养的微视频教学实施 ·············· 154

第七章
初中英语微课堂教学研究成果及反思 ·············· 173

附 录 ·············· 180
参考文献 ·············· 183

第一章

「微课」在英语教学中的应用

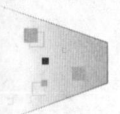

"微课"在初中英语课堂教学中的应用初探

一、"微课"背景

(一)国外背景

美国北爱荷华大学(University of Northern Iowa)LeRoy A. McGrew教授所提出的60秒课程(60-Second Course)(McGrew,1993)以及英国纳皮尔大学(Napier University)T. P. Kee提出的一分钟演讲(The One Minute Lecture,简称OML)是微课程的雏形。

现今热议的微课程(Micro-lecture)概念是在2008年由美国新墨西哥州圣胡安学院的高级教学设计师、学院在线服务经理David Penrose提出的。Penrose提出建设微课程的五个步骤:罗列课堂教学中试图传递的核心概念,这些核心概念将构成微课程的核心;写出一份15~30秒的介绍和总结,为核心概念提供上下文背景;用麦克风或网络摄像头录制以上内容,最终的节目长度为1~3分钟;设计能够指导学生阅读或探索的课后任务,帮助学生学习课程材料的内容;将教学视频与课程任务上传到课程管理系统。在公开的微课程中做得比较成功的是可汗学院(Khan Academy)和TED-Ed。

(二)国内背景

在中国,广东省佛山市教育局胡铁生基于现有教育信息资源利用率低的现状,率先提出了以微视频为中心的新型教学资源——"微课"。"微课"的核心内容是课堂教学视频(课例片段),同时还包含与该教学主题相关的教学设计、素材课件、教学反思、练习测试及学生反馈、教师点评等教学支持资源。

华南师范大学与凤凰卫视集团联手推出"微课",6000多个网络视频课程

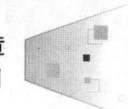

免费开放。在内容制作方面，华南师大携手凤凰卫视将教学资源与媒体资源相整合，运用新媒体技术对视频内容进行二次开发，使之为各种移动终端提供内容服务。

（三）教学背景

实验学校是广东省东莞市的一所镇办初中，据不完全统计，在2010—2014年期间，每年有100多名优秀学生通过自主招生考试到市优质民办学校就读，导致留在镇中学的优质生源越来越少。在2014年，学校有48个教学班，共25位英语教师。该校英语教师的现状：①教师年龄偏大，英语科组教师平均年龄41.2岁，50岁以上的教师有7人，最年轻的教师教龄也有7年了；②高中教师教初中，该校原是一所完全中学，2007年撤了高中部后，部分原高中教师分流到初中，不适应或者说还未完全适应初中的教学。各种因素导致班与班之间的成绩差距较大。这样的状况，加上优质民办学校学位的冲击，学校英语教学一直处于非常被动的状态，总是被学校和学生牵着走。各年级期末参加市统测英语成绩都低于市平均分4~6分，其他科与市平均分的差距更大，一直无法突破这个瓶颈。因此，2012年学校成了东莞市教育局指定的第一批被帮扶学校。适逢2014年初东莞市教研室开始在全市开展微课的开发与研究，因此开展"初中英语课堂微视频的设计与实施"的研究，通过教学研究促进教学，突破英语教学瓶颈。

二、教学意义

综观目前关于"微课"的研究，主要集中在以网络在线课程和非正式学习的领域。而对于"微课"运用于课堂教学的可行性及如何实施微课程的研究比较少，这说明本研究是有必要的，而且可以有所创新和发展。目前已有的研究为本研究对于初中英语微技能视频设计模式提供了很好的理论和实践基础，也提高了本研究的可行性。

（一）教师方面

1. 有利于优质资源的共享

教学微视频既有别于传统单一资源类型的教学课例、教学课件、教学设计、教学反思等教学资源，又是在其基础上继承和发展起来的一种新型教学资源，是微课程的核心教学资源。当一个优质的教学微视频录制成功以后，所有学生都能够通过移动终端得到最优质的教学资源，随时随地为学生或教师提供参考，这对优质教学资源不均衡的地区而言尤为重要。

2. 有助于教师专业发展

教师要把一个教学知识点讲得清楚透彻，没有严密的思维、专业的教学设计是无法录制出吸引人的微视频。为了让微视频更有创意、更新颖，教师往往是提出一个设想，否定，再提出一个，再否定，如此反复，甚至视频的录制也是经过多次的修改剪辑。就在这些反复修改的过程中，视频制作者的专业水平不断地提高，录制越多，越有经验，越娴熟。

3. 有助于创新课程教学模式

单一的、习惯的教学模式让学生觉得枯燥无味，传统的训练也没有目的性。在课堂上，借助微视频的帮助，让学生通过不一样的教学模式来学习新的知识或技能，也是一种尝试和创新。

4. 有助于发挥骨干教师的引领作用

研究成员通过设计微视频，并尝试在课堂教学中运用，成功的经验可以在学校英语科组推广，甚至推广到全市。

（二）学生方面

1. 有助于进行个性化学习

教学视频内容精悍，不同的学生可以根据自己的实际学习情况选取不同的视频进行学习，视频的时间短，还可以重复播放，使学生可以自控地进行深度学习，满足不同的学生需求，获得个性化的体验。

2. 作为"补救式"教学手段

如果学生由于某些原因而错过教师课堂上的讲授、同学的帮助，没有掌握到某知识点，课后，可以观看教学微视频，有针对性地对该知识点进行学习、掌握和巩固。缺课的学生在课后观看微视频进行自主学习，属于"补救式"教学，教学微视频在其中可以发挥其个性化的、自主学习的作用。

3. 有助于家长了解学生的学习情况

教师课堂上使用的微视频，可以分享给学生或者家长，让家长监督并及时了解学生的学习情况。

三、理论依据

《教育信息化十年发展规划（2011—2020年）》指出，教育信息化的发展要以教育理念创新为先导，以优质教育资源和信息化学习环境建设为基础，以学习方式和教育模式创新为核心。

《基础教育课程改革纲要》指出，要大力推进信息技术在教学过程中的普遍应用，促进信息技术与学科课程的整合，逐步实现教学内容的呈现方式、学生的学习方式、教师的教学方式和师生互动方式的变革，充分发挥信息技术的优势，为学生的学习和发展提供丰富多彩的教育环境和有力的学习工具。

《英语课程标准》（2011年版）指出，语言学习需要大量的输入。丰富多样的课程资源对英语学习尤其重要。英语课程应根据教和学的需求，提供贴近学生、贴近生活、贴近时代的英语学习资源，创造性地开发和利用现实生活中鲜活的英语学习资源，积极利用音像、广播、电视、书报杂志、网络信息等，拓展学生学习和运用英语的渠道。

因此，学校应开始进行探究教学微视频的设计以及微视频在初中英语日常课堂教学中的实际应用。

四、研究目标

本研究尝试以微技能视频作为切入点，探究微技能视频运用于初中英语常规课堂教学中的有效性。通过微视频的设计和开展教育教研活动，推广微技能视频的实施，从而提高课堂效率。

具体目标如下：

（1）探索"微视频"模式。

（2）构建适合课堂教学使用的微视频资源库。

（3）探索以微技能视频提高课堂效率和教学效果的可行性途径和方法。

五、研究的主要内容

（1）听力技能的视频设计与实施。

（2）阅读技能的视频设计与实施。

（3）专题语法的视频设计与实施。

（4）话题写作视频的设计与实施。

（5）文化意识微视频的设计与实施。

六、核心概念的界定

本研究以常态教学为载体，根据研究的具体内容分别采用不同的方法来开展研究活动和研讨课，主要的研究方法是行动研究法，同时还有案例研究法、调查研究法、文献研究法等。

1. 核心概念

本研究的核心概念是"微视频（Micro-video）"，优酷网原总裁古永锵指出："微视频（又称视频分享类短片）是指个体通过PC、手机、摄像头、DV、DC、MP4等多种视频终端摄录、上传互联网进而播放共享的短则30秒、长则20分钟左右的内容广泛、形态多样，涵盖小电影、纪录短片、DV短片、视频剪辑、广告片段等视频短片的统称。其中，短、快、精、大众参与性、随时随地随意性是微视频最大的特点 。"教学微视频最早源于翻转课堂，在美国的可汗学院和林地公园高中的翻转课堂模式中，教学视频承担着知识传授的责任，其质量对知识传授的效果有着重要的影响。而本研究所指的微视频主要包括微课（Micro-course）和微视频片段（Micro-video clips）两种。

（1）"微课"，是以教学视频为主要呈现方式，经过精心的信息化教学设计，以多媒体形式展示的围绕某个知识点或教学环节开展的简短教学活动。其核心资源是"微视频"（教学视频片段），同时还包含与该教学主题相关的"微教案""微课件""微习题""微反思"等辅助性教学内容。其特点在于：①短而精，主要表现为知识内容少，视频长度短（5~10分钟）和数据量小；②目标明确，即教学目标单一，主题突出，教学指向明确；③易于分享和交流。

（2）微视频片段主要指从电影、DV等视频中根据教学需求剪辑加工的1~5分钟的视频片段，其主要作用是辅助教学。

2. 问卷调查

通过问卷调查，分析调查结果，也就是对东莞市镇办初中英语课堂教学技能现状进行调查，分析原因，对微技能视频教学的可行性进行调查判断（调查问卷和统计结果详见附录）。

3. 设计制作微课

巧妙地设计微课教学活动，能够有效地激发学生的学习兴趣，提高学生的学习效果。设计一节好的微课，应遵循以下原则：

（1）选择和分析处理知识点。知识点尽量选热门的考点、教学的重点、难点；知识点的选择要细，8分钟内能讲透彻；知识点要准确，没有知识性错误或误导性描述；要将知识点按一定逻辑分割成多个小知识点，例如，《现在完成时的"短"与"延"》《听力微技能之记笔记》等。

（2）选择合适的微课类型。根据所要讲解的知识点选择适当的微课类型，有助于提高微课堂的效果，比如，听力技能微视频、专题语法微视频等。

（3）构建完整精练的教学过程。切入课题要新颖、迅速；讲授线索要鲜明；结尾要快捷；力求创新，亮点耀眼。

（4）制作实用的微课教学课件。教学课件能充分创造出一个图文并茂、有声有色、生动逼真的教学环境，为教师教学的顺利实施提供形象的表达工具，能有效地突破教学难点，激发学生的学习兴趣，真正改变传统教学单调的模式，使乐学落到实处。因此，制作微课课件要注意以下几点：具有美感；动静结合；合理安排信息量；易于操作。

（5）制作微视频。设计好教学课件，就可以运用电脑软件进行视频的录制，我们主要使用的软件有CS6录屏软件、会声会影、格式工厂等。

4. 制作优课

学科研究的课例研讨是学科研究过程中不断发现、判断和提升研究质量与价值的重要活动，是研究和成果转化的一个重要环节。把研讨课的微视频、教学课件、教学设计、课堂实录以及教学反思和课堂练习等辅助性教学内容汇集，制作成优课资源，可以作为微视频在初中英语课堂实施的课例。

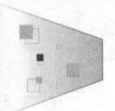

玩转英语课堂的微视频
——初中英语课堂微视频的设计与实施

"微课"在初中英语课堂教学中的应用优势

新课程改革对初中英语课堂教学成效提出了更高的要求,"微课"作为一种以视频为主要载体的新型教学模式,是教师针对某一教学环节或某个知识点而实施的有关教与学的有机整合,具有教学内容丰富、教学目标清晰明确、教学过程循序渐进以及知识点积少成多等诸多优势。将"微课"积极地运用于初中英语课堂教学中,不仅能够有力地突破传统初中英语课堂教学的时空局限,而且能够有效激发学生的学习兴趣,帮助学生深刻理解文本内容并高效解决英语疑难,还能够充分发挥学生在学习中的主体地位和教师在教学中的主导地位,从而提升初中英语课堂教学的实效性,最终实现"自主学习、快乐学习、高效学习"。当前,"微课"在初中英语课堂教学中的应用优势主要体现在以下几方面。

一、激发学生的学习兴趣

众所周知,兴趣是学生最好的老师。要想显著地提升学生的英语水平,广大初中英语教师必须积极采取多种途径来激发学生对英语这门语言学科的学习兴趣。相比于传统"满堂灌"式的教学模式,"微课"具有短小精悍、生动有趣的鲜明特性,被视为激发学生课堂兴趣的一大法宝。

例如,在人教版九年级英语"Unit 10 You are supposed to shake hands."中,基于本单元的中心话题customs in different countries,在课堂伊始,为了快速引导学生进入学习状态,首先向学生展示了一段自己精心制作的不同国家初次见面的礼仪的微视频,在进入知识点讲授之前首先让学生怀着愉悦的心情观看这段图片、文字、音乐多元结合的微视频,瞬间点燃学生的学习热情,从而让学生快速进入学习情境中，让学生以一种情绪激昂、精力旺盛的学习状态参与到后续的教学活动中。同时，也让学生感知各国的习俗与文化，增强学生英语学习中的跨文化意识。

二、创设教学情境

在初中英语课堂教学过程中，教学情境的有效创设是决定课堂教学成效的重要因素之一，而"微课"特有的情景性与场景性往往十分吸引学生的眼球，具有开阔视野、拓展思维的作用，能够让学生在身临其境中聚焦问题、思考问题。

例如，在人教版九年级英语"Unit 13 We're trying to save the earth."的第二课时，为了让学生了解一些濒临灭绝的动物的生活习性和濒临灭绝的原因，教育学生如何保护环境，为了完成培养学生环保意识的情感教育目标，设计了以下几段微视频。

第一段：Before class, ask students to search for information and pictures about endangered animals. Then ask students to make a video in groups of six and show the video to the class, every video is less than 2 minutes. 课前，要求学生通过各种媒体搜集有关濒危动物的英文介绍和相关图片，分组制作微视频，然后课堂上与学生交流展示每组制作的视频，每段视频不超过2分钟。

第二段：Let Students see a video about sharks together and get students to know something about the sharks. 教师播放鲨鱼的录像，让学生对鲨鱼的形象有更直观的认知，并进一步介绍有关鲨鱼的现状。

第三段：Show a video about why sharks are becoming endangered. Then ask students to save sharks and other animals! 多媒体展示人类捕杀鲨鱼及其他动物的照片，告诉学生鲨鱼正面临着灭绝的危险，呼吁全体同学一起来拯救濒危动物！

通过适时地加入微视频，在直观的、颇具震撼力的画面面前，学生们的心灵触动颇深，对保护环境，尤其是保护和拯救濒危动物有了更加深刻的认识。

三、拓展学生思维

英语作为一门语言类学科，学生不可避免地要学习诸多语法知识，而有些语法项目包含的内容较多，学生在实际运用过程中容易出现张冠李戴、混淆不清的现象。为了帮助学生形成清晰、系统的知识网络体系，有效拓展学生思维，将微课应用于思维导图教学中，往往会取得事半功倍之效。

例如，在一次九年级复习观摩课上，只用短短一节课的时间完成了定语从句、状语从句、宾语从句、感叹句以及反义疑问句的回顾与总结，这样大容量信息的知识复习，正是基于"微课"与思维导图的高效运用。

首先借助Mind Map软件做出本节课内容的思维导图，然后根据导图之间的相互联系依次展示微课程，让整个教学过程变得条理清晰、直观明了。此外，在课后给学生布置了任务，让同学们仿照微课中思维导图的展示过程，画出属于自己的思维导图。通过对该学习模式的模仿，学生不仅高效梳理了语法之间的关系，深化了理解，而且将原本隐形的思维过程变得直观明了，在回顾知识点的过程中很好地拓展了个人思维。

四、开发学生潜能

对于正处于身心发展旺盛期的中学生而言，他们有着强大的开发潜能。通过引导学生自行动手制作"微课"，不仅可以开辟新的学习渠道，而且极大地开发了学生潜能，很好地锻炼了学生的动手能力、合作能力、创新能力等。

例如，在教授人教版八年级上册"Unit 8 How do you make a banana milk shake？"这一课时。为了引导学生熟练运用"How much..." "How many..." 来对数量提问，有效攻克"恰当使用祈使句表达食物的制作过程"这一教学难点，有力地培养学生的实际生活能力，在完成Unit 8的教学后布置了这样一道"微课"制作任务：请同学们以小组为单位（2~3人一组），合作制作一段"如何做一道美食"的微视频，并将完成的美食带至课堂分享。其中某一小组就"How to make the Double-layer Steamed Milk"做了一段美食制作视频，总结出了Double-layer Steamed Milk的主要制作过程："First, we need two eggs and milk; Then, put the eggs and milk into a bowl; Next, add the sugar in the bowl;

After that, cook for 25 minutes; Finally, you can eat it."该小组所带来的Double-layer Steamed Milk也获得了全班学生的一致好评。具体如下图所示。

How to make the Double-layer Steamed Milk

First, we need two eggs and milk.

Then, put the eggs and milk into a bowl.

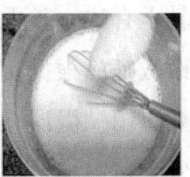
Next, add the sugar in the bowl.

After that, cook for 25 minutes.

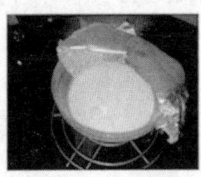
Finally, you can eat it.

By 温维　张锦城
　　邓振邦

总之，通过小组合作完成制作美食的微视频，不仅高效地突破了教学的难点，而且很好地培养了学生实际生活、实际操作以及实际动手的能力，还让学生真实体会到劳动成果的来之不易，于合作中制作，于制作中创新，有力地激发了学生的潜能。

五、促进资源共享

教学改革对英语教学资源提出了更高的要求，而将"微课"积极引入和高效应用至初中英语课堂，有力地促进优秀教学资源的共享，每一位老师都能够汲取其中的精华，为己所用，从而显著提升初中英语课堂教学的质量与成效。近年来，东莞市教育局每年都会举办"微课"比赛，通过与优秀同行之间的友好切磋和积极交流，分享到许多优秀、精彩的教学资源，将其运用到日常课堂教学中，受到了学生的一致好评。例如，在讲授语法知识点时，适时加入一些关于语法的"微课"，并将其上传至班级群内。一方面，学生能够感受到不同老师的上课风格，给学生带来巨大的新鲜感和兴趣，使枯燥的语法变得生动，让人印象深刻；另一方面，水平较差的学生可在班级群内下载"微课"，在家反复观看复习，夯实基础。

六、结语

总之，教学有法，教无定法。无论哪一种教学模式，都有其长处与短处。广大初中英语教师应根据实际教学要求和学生的实际学习情况，精心编排、合理设计和高效运用"微课"，充分发挥"微课"在初中英语课堂教学中的应用优势——激发学习兴趣、创设教学情境、拓展学生思维、开发学生潜能以及促进资源共享，从而最大限度地发挥"微课"在初中英语课堂教学中的效用，打造快乐、高效、优质的初中英语课堂。

第二章

听力技能的微视频设计与实施

初中英语课堂听力技能微视频实施的必要性

一、听力技能

John Field 在解释外语听力理解和教学过程时引进了听力技能（listening skills）这个概念。根据他的界定，听力技能（listening skills）是母语听者既已掌握而外语听者要习得的能力（aptitudes/competence）。它们涉及对语音的感知能力（mastering the auditory phonetics）、辨词能力（mastering the word-identification techniques）、掌握推理的方式（mastering the patterns of reference）和目标语中信息的分配（mastering the distribution of information which occur in the target language）。初中阶段的听力理解技能主要包括以下五种：听细节（listening for details）、听主旨大意（listening for gist）、推论（drawing inferences）、选听（listening selectively）和预测（making predictions）。具体到日常教学中，最常用的听力理解技能的设计模式有听前活动brainstorming, mind-mapping, discussion, games, guiding questions, pictures/diagrams, questions or prediction；听时活动sound discrimination, guessing new words or note-taking；听后活动multiple choice, note-taking, true or false, matching, answer questions, complete sentences, dictation, write a short summary等。

二、听力的重要性

任何人要想掌握一门语言，都必须先听懂这门语言，只有在这个基础之上，才能够很好地了解他人所表达的思想，并将自己所要表达的思想与看法表达出来。根据美国外语教学法专家里弗斯（Wilga M.Rivers）和坦珀利

第二章
听力技能的微视频设计与实施

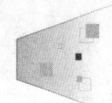

（M.S.Temperly）的统计，听在人类交际活动中所占的比例为45%，居听、说、读、写各语言活动之首。通过这一研究数据我们不难发现，"听"是语言的基础。基于这样的情况，我们在开展初中英语教学时，就必须重视听力教学。因为听力不但是说、读、写的基础，更是提高教学质量与效率的重要保证。因此，要想更好地提高初中英语教学的质量，全面实现英语教学的目标，更好地提高学生的英语水平，我们就必须重视听力教学。

《英语课程标准》对初中阶段听力技能教学的要求是：教师要准确定位教学目标，宏观把握教学设计的依据，全面了解各学段的目标，使自己在教学设计中能更好地、更准确地把握。在东莞市初中阶段升学考试试题中，120分的满分卷，其中口语占12分，笔试中听力部分占25分，也就是说，涉及听力理解的分数比重为31%。

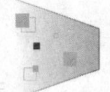
玩转英语课堂的微视频
——初中英语课堂微视频的设计与实施

初中英语课堂听力技能微视频实施的可行性

一、问卷调查

为了更深入地了解目前初中阶段英语课堂中微视频运用的教学情况，随机选取东莞市8所镇办初中三个年级的152名英语老师参加了此次问卷调查，问卷设计了10个问题，有单项和多项选择。问题的设计如下：

关于在英语课堂中利用微视频进行教学的问卷调查

1. 您任教的年级为_____
2. 您尝试过在英语课堂中利用微视频进行教学吗？（　　）
   A. 经常　　　　　　　B. 偶尔　　　　　　　C. 从不
3. 您觉得微视频的长度在多少分钟比较合适？（　　）
   A. 3～5分钟　　　　　B. 5～10分钟　　　　 C. 10～15分钟
4. 您通过哪种方式获得微视频？（可多选）（　　）
   A. 同事提供　　　　　B. 书商提供　　　　　C. 网上下载
   D. 剪辑加工　　　　　E. 原创
5. 您认为用微视频进行课堂教学方便吗？（　　）
   A. 方便　　　　　　　B. 不方便　　　　　　C. 不清楚
6. 您尝试过制作微视频吗？（　　）
   A. 经常　　　　　　　B. 偶尔　　　　　　　C. 从不
7. 您认为教师参与微视频使用的积极性高吗？（　　）
   A. 高　　　　　　　　B. 一般　　　　　　　C. 不高

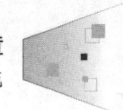

8. 您身边在英语课堂上使用微视频的老师多吗？（　　）

　　A. 多　　　　　　　B. 一般　　　　　　　C. 没有

9. 您的同事课堂上使用微视频对您有促进吗？（　　）

　　A. 有　　　　　　　B. 一般　　　　　　　C. 没有

10. 您认为目前微视频的种类还可以增加哪些？（可多选）（　　）

　　A. 语法类　　　　　　B. 词汇类

　　C. 阅读技能类　　　　D. 听力技能类

　　E. 写作指导类　　　　F. 文化背景类

　　G. 不清楚

调查结果显示，在参加问卷调查的老师中，41%的教师从来没有在英语课堂中利用过微视频进行教学，49%的教师认为微视频的长度在5~10分钟比较合适，63%的教师直接使用网上下载的微视频，62%的教师认为微视频使用方便，49%的教师从未尝试过制作微视频，11%的教师认为身边的同事使用微视频对自己没有促进。

由此可见，东莞市目前英语教师对微视频的了解是比较浅的，运用得也比较少。而随着教育资源的丰富、教育交流的方便、学校教学设备的不断完善，在初中英语课堂上探索微视频的设计并尝试运用于课堂教学是可行的，对课堂也有一定的促进作用。

二、听力技能微视频教学的优劣

听力技能微视频运用于课堂上，不仅能起到活跃课堂气氛的作用，也让课堂有耳目一新的变化。

（1）能够进行系列性的听力技巧指导。把听力各种微技能以单一或组合等形式制作成微视频，有目的地对学生进行指导。

（2）能够进行有针对性的听力指导。有针对性的听力指导对九年级中考题型复习有很大帮助。

（3）让学生接触不同题材的听力材料。学生平时接触的听力材料有限，通过微视频，可以扩充学生听力材料的题材。

但是，在进行微视频教学探索的时候，也应该清楚地认识到以下一些不足：

(1）教学微视频不能替代教师。教学微视频应该是在教师的推动下，学生进行有序的、互助的学习。但学生需要指导时，教师要向他们提供必要的支持。

（2）教学微视频只能作为一种教学手段。教学微视频的应用应该是为了创设更多的机会让学生进行学习，创新学习形式，让学习多样化。

（3）教学微视频不能替代传统教学。教学微视频只是提高教学质量的途径之一，它不是教学的全部，对于大部分学生仍然存疑的部分，还是需要教师进行讲解。

初中英语课堂听力技能微视频实施的教学案例

一、听力技能微视频的设计

1. 微设计

基于以上调查，以"听力微技能"为主题设计了一节微课，尝试在七年级开始对学生进行听力技能的培养与训练，微课的设计如下表所示。

听力技能微视频的设计

微课基本信息	知识点名称	听力微技能
	教学对象	七年级学生
	预计上课时间长度	8分钟
教学目标： 掌握听力理解的预测、听主旨大意、听细节、推论和选听五种微技能。		
教学资源与环境： PC终端，平板电脑，移动终端。		
教学过程： 1. 观察归纳：预测的途径。 2. 听主旨大意的问题设计。 3. 听细节的方法。 4. 推论的题目。 5. 选听和小结。		
设计理念与特色： 本节微课主要把完成一项综合性活动所需的各种过程和能力化整为零，逐一讲解，一一击破，化难为易。		
微课制作方式： CS录屏软件+声音。		

2. 微课件

录制本节微课,所用到的PPT设计如下图所示:

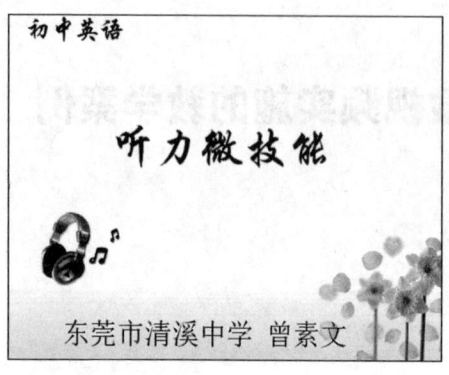

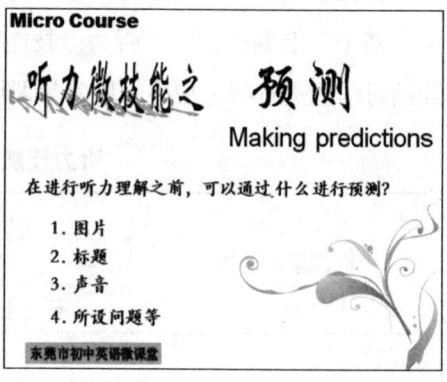
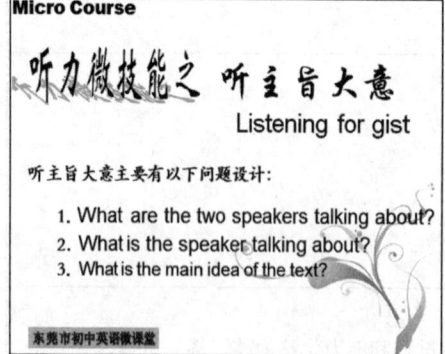
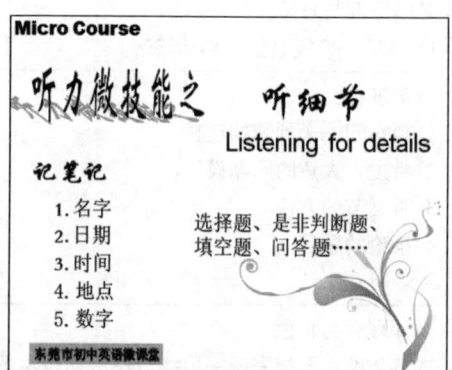

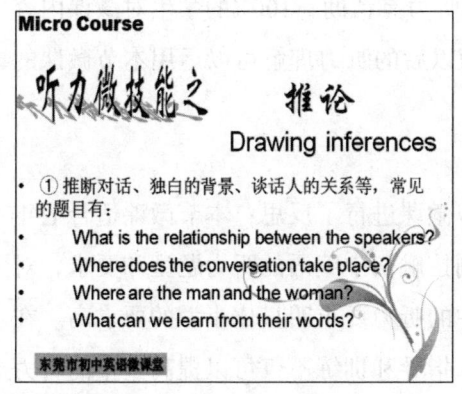

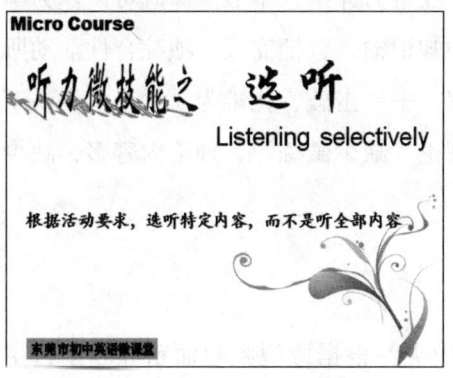
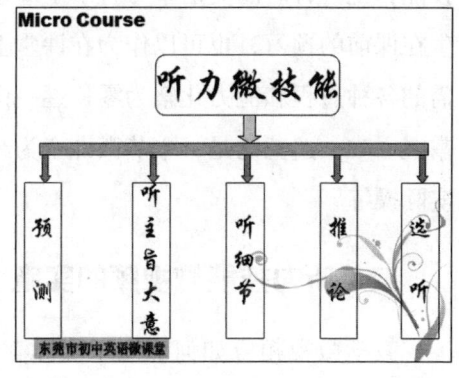

3. 微调查

对于这个微视频，在观看后还设计了问卷调查，调查内容如下：

关于"听力微技能"微课问卷调查

1. 你认为本节微课的长度合适吗？（　　）

　　A. 合适　　　　　　B. 太长　　　　　　C. 太短

2. 你认为本节微课的内容对本节听力课有帮助吗？（　　）

　　A. 有　　　　　　　B. 没有

3. 你能理解微课内容的多少？（　　）

　　A. 90%～100%　　B. 80%～90%　　C. 70%～80%　　D. 60%以下

4. 你在以后的听力理解中能运用本节微课的内容吗？（　　）

　　A. 能　　　　　　　B. 不能

调查结果显示，学生对这节微课的设计比较满意：75%的学生认为微课的长度合适，98%的学生认为微课的内容对听力有帮助，100%的学生对微课内容的理解选择90%～100%，87%的学生认为以后的听力理解可以运用本节微课的内容。

4. 微反思

根据微课设计和学生调查，我对本节微课进行了反思：本节微课适合七年级学生进行听力技能训练。七年级学生刚接触初中英语的听力题型和要求，对听力理解的掌握没有系统的训练，而初中的听力要求明显比小学的要求高。在这样的情况下，对学生进行听力微技能的指导和训练不仅可以提高学生的听力技能，也为日后的英语学习打下了基础。在听力课中，本节微课既可以作为学生在课前的预习，也可以作为在课堂上的知识输入，把完成一项综合性活动所需的各种过程和能力化整为零，逐一讲解，一一击破，化难为易，让学生易于掌握。唯一遗憾的是，本节微课全为纯理论，缺少微练习，理论内容多，缺少实际操练。

二、听力技能微视频的实施

教学微视频应如何应用于实际教学中呢？根据微视频短而精和利于自主学习的特点，基于其在教学中的辅助作用，可以把微视频分为Pre-Micro-video, While-Micro-video 和 Post-Micro-video三种。

1. Pre-Micro-video（课前微视频）

在初中英语学习中，会有不少知识点或技能技巧是学生比较容易掌握的、一看就懂的，如果在学生接触这些内容之前，教师提前布置学习任务，让学生自行观看相关的微视频，通过微视频的观看可以达到预先学习的效果。当然，教师布置观看任务的同时也应该布置检测观看结果的任务以评价学生的预习成果。有了这种微视频学习作为铺垫，课堂上再进行教学与反馈就得心应手了。

2. While-Micro-video（课中微视频）

相对于系统的学习，在日常的英语课堂教学中，我们还经常遇到一些额外的知识插入，如在综合课上遇到听力理解、在复习课上遇到语法知识点等，此时，如果在课堂上播放相关的教学微视频，既可以通过改变授课形式调节课堂的沉闷、活跃课堂气氛，也减轻了教师的授课负担，同时达到优质资源的共享。

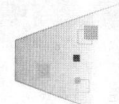

3. Post-Micro-video（课后微视频）

课后微视频也有利于学生的自主学习。每位学生对不同知识点的掌握程度都不同，如果教师把同一个知识点反反复复地讲解，对于已经掌握的学生来说就是浪费时间，炒冷饭。那么对于还不懂的学生怎么办呢？不讲解不行。那么，课后学生可以根据自己的理解水平，选择所需的微视频进行"补救式"的复习巩固，以达到自己的学习目的。

根据上述的微视频设计，尝试在七年级学生听力课上播放微视频（While-Micro-video），通过微视频的辅助，提高课堂效率。听力课教学流程示意图设计如下图所示。

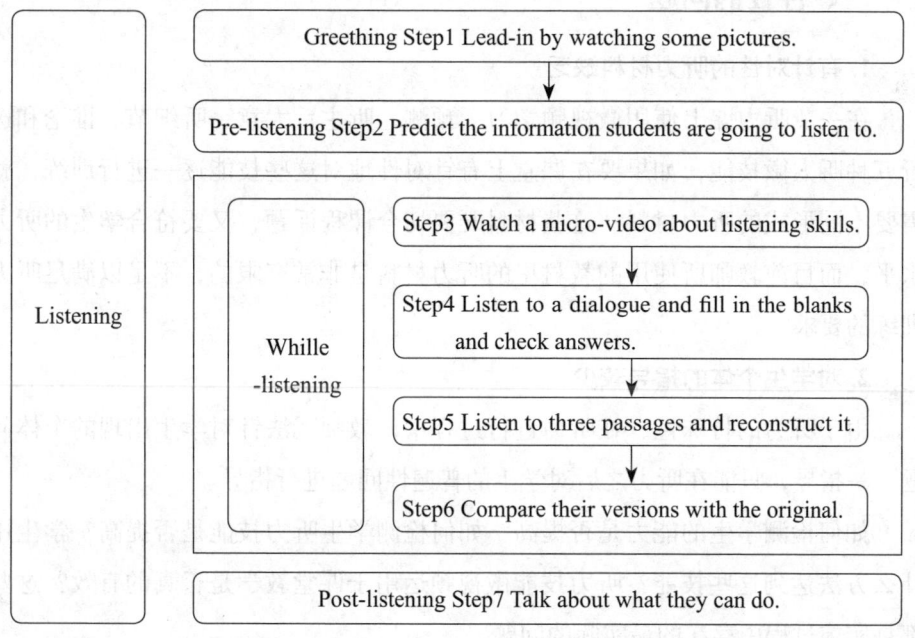

本节听力课在选材上主要考虑了以下方面：材料的真实性、交际性；材料中的语速属于自然语速；材料提供能让学生感兴趣和能激发学生学习动机的语境。在教学环节的设计上，则大胆地在听前活动中插入了微视频的观看，通过观看微视频来学习听力微技能，然后再针对各微技能进行听力训练，目的是让学生学会运用微技能来提高自身的听力水平。本节听力课是对信息化教学的一个很好的尝试，在对学生进行听力技能的指导，训练学生能力的同时，也培养了学生的自学能力。

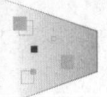
玩转英语课堂的微视频
——初中英语课堂微视频的设计与实施

初中英语课堂听力技能微视频实施的问题和对策

一、存在的问题

1. 有针对性的听力材料缺乏

在一节听力课上使用微视频学习了预测、听主旨大意、听细节、推论和选听五种听力微技能，如果要在课堂上有针对性地对这些技能逐一进行训练，就需要不同形式的听力材料。这些材料既要切合课程话题，又要符合学生的听力水平，而目前教师所使用的教材里的听力材料是非常有限的，不足以满足听力训练的要求。

2. 对学生个体的指导较少

由于听力的特殊性，在听力进行过程中，教师无法针对学生出现的个体问题一一指导，只能在听力之后对学生的普遍性问题进行指导。

如何检测学生的能力是否提高？如何检测学生听力技能是否提高？学生用什么方法达到这些技能？听力技能微视频运用于课堂教学是否真的有效？这些都是实施过程中存在的最实际的问题。

二、解决的对策

1. 对于听力训练材料的选取，应该遵循使用英语原声材料的原则

通过英美网站搜索适合学生听力水平的听力材料，比如，上述案例中的一个对话：

Boy: Ah, band auditions. Great! I'd love to be in a band! ... Hi. Is this the band audition?

Girl: Hello. Yes. So, you'd like to be in our band?

Boy: Yes, I love music.

Girl: Well, we need a singer, a guitarist and a drummer.

Boy: Oh, I love singing!

Girl: OK, so you can sing. Let's sing the beginning of this song.

Boy: (singing) Tonight I'm going to have myself a real good time. I feel alive ...

Girl: Right, OK, mmm, maybe not. Can you play an instrument?

Boy: Er, well, I can play the guitar a little.

Girl: OK, let's hear you. What can you play? ... That's it?

Boy: Er, yeah. I can't remember any more.

Girl: Erm, can you play the drums?

Boy: Yeah, sure.

Girl: OK! OK! STOP! That's enough. Erm, what about the maracas? Can you play the maracas?

Boy: Yes, I can. (singing) Young and strong and ... er ...

Girl: Great, great! Hmm ... thanks for coming. I'll call you next week.

这个对话情景性强，话题新颖，容易引起学生的兴趣，能够作为听力材料运用于课堂上，对学生听力技能的提高有很大帮助。另外，还可以考虑使用不同教材的听力材料。比如，东莞市使用的是人教版的教材，那我们就可以通过广州市的沪教版教材或其他城市不同版本的教材，根据《英语课程标准》话题项目，选用教材里面的难度及话题类似的配音材料。这无疑是一种新的尝试，如下表所示（以七年级上册为例）。

七年级上册教材配音材料

Topics	人教版	沪教版
Interests and hobbies	Unit 1 Can you play the guitar?	Module 4 Fun time
Daily life	Unit 2 What time do you go to school?	Unit 2 Daily life
Travel and transport	Unit 3 How do you get to school? Unit 11 How was your school trip? Unit 12 What did you do last weekend?	Module 3 Travel

续表

Topics	人教版	沪教版
Family, friends and people around	Unit 9 What does he look like?	Unit 1 Making friends
Weather	Unit 7 It's raining.	Unit 4 Seasons

2. 要关注对不同层次学生在听力微技能上的指导

根据学生的知识水平，在听前、听中或听后活动上做文章，尽量设计有层次的活动模式，以满足不同层次学生的要求。在课后，积极设计不同形式的问卷调查，收集学生对课堂的反馈，以便对不同学生进行针对性的指导。

3. 学生的听力水平，非一朝一夕之功

首先，要确定实验班和实验学生，与非实验班进行对比；其次，要对这些学生进行跟踪测试，每实验一个阶段进行一次测试，通过测试结果的分析来对比实验结果的优劣。例如，在东莞市清溪中学的七年级学生中进行实验，实验班学生为七年级（7）（8）班，共93人，非实验班学生为七年级（5）（6）班，共97人，以上学期期末统考的英语听力成绩为原始成绩，本学期开始在这些班中每个星期进行一次听力测试，如下表所示。

测试结果的对比

	期末测试	第1周	第2周	第3周	第4周	第5周	第6周	第7周	第8周	第9周	第10周	第11周	第12周	平均值
非实验班	82%	88%	92%	96%	80%	60%	68%	80%	72%	64%	72%	68%	76%	83%
实验班	84%	92%	92%	96%	92%	76%	76%	84%	72%	72%	76%	80%	80%	89%

根据以上数据，可知在实验班进行听力技能的培养和训练，经过12周的测试，学生的听力成绩与非实验班学生相比，是有区别的，特别体现在难度大的题型上。

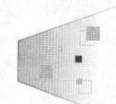

教学实践与事实证明，是否注重学生听力技能的培养和训练对学生听力成绩有明显影响。本文着重探讨了听力技能微视频在课堂上的运用，影响听力的因素是多方面的，听力技能也是多样的，不同的技能在不同的学习者身上会产生不同的效果。这就要求学习者要具体情况具体分析，根据自身的学习特点，培养和训练适合自己的技能技巧。

一、听力微技能之记笔记微课设计脚本

1. 基本信息

基本信息

微课名称	听力微技能之记笔记	微课类型	听力微技能
授课/制作人	郑艳霞	制作方式	CS录屏软件+PPT
适用对象	初二学生	时长	8分钟
教学目标	本节微课通过介绍缩略词的4种记录方法与13种常见的数学符号和标点符号的记录方法来教会学生快速记录。		
创新与亮点	本节微课的创新与亮点在于，通过一些简单的记笔记的方法引导学生琢磨适合自己的记录方法，微课所列举的方法仅起抛砖引玉的作用，不是唯一的，让学生学会快速记录才是目的。		

2. 设计与录制脚本

设计与录制脚本

教学步骤/活动	教学语言表述内容	多媒体配合方式与设计意图
Greeting & Learning goals	T: 欢迎进入东莞市初中英语微课堂，我是清溪中学曾素文。本节微课主要学习听力微技能之记笔记。	多媒体配合方式：PPT 第1~3页。设计意图：明确作者与本节课的学习内容。
What to write down	S: 那记笔记都记录什么呢？ T: 记笔记主要记录名字、时间、地点、日期、数字和关键词等。	多媒体配合方式：PPT第4页。设计意图：介绍要记录的笔记内容。

续 表

教学 步骤/活动	教学语言表述内容	多媒体配合方式 与设计意图
How to write quickly	1. 快速记录 S：听录音时要边听边记录，会不会手忙脚乱？ T：这就是我们这节微课的目的了，我们要学会快速记录。首先，边听边记录非常重要。其次，记录并不是说必须记下每个单词，而是将能帮助理解听力内容的关键信息记录下来。 2. 缩略词 T：另外，还有窍门哦。我们要学会运用缩略词。第一类，拿掉单词中所有元音，如MKT表示market, MSG表示message, 来试一下吧！ S：Ok. T：What did you write down? S：VLG and SM. 用VLG 表示village，用SM表示summer. T：第二类缩略词，保留单词前几个字母，如用info表示information, IOU表示I owe you.等，Have a try! T：Show me your notes! S：1 ora, 3 ham, 5 chi. T：Right, don't forget the numbers! T：第三类缩略词，保留单词开头和结尾发音的字母，如用WK表示week、用RM表示room, Let's go! S：No problem! T：Now, let's see! S：30, CL4, 26, CLM. T：Well done! 第四类缩略词，根据单词的发音，如用字母R表示are, 用字母U表示you. S：It's a piece of cake! 3. 数学符号和标点符号 T：除此之外，我们还可以借助数学符号和标点符号来进行快速记录。 S：Oh, tell me! T：用+表示多，如many, lots of, a great deal of; 用- 表示少，如little, few; 用×表示错误、失误、坏，如wrong, bad; 用>表示多于、高、超过，如bigger, better, morethan; 用< 表示少于、低于，如less, smaller; 用= 表示等同、对手，如means, the same as; 用（　）表示在……之间，如among,	多媒体配合方式： PPT第5～15页。 设计意图： 1. 介绍快速记录的方法。 2. 介绍四种缩略词的运用。 3. 介绍13种常见的数学符号和标点符号。

续 表

教学步骤/活动	教学语言表述内容	多媒体配合方式与设计意图
How to write quickly	within；用≠表示不同、无敌，如be different from，peerless；用≈表示大约，如about, around, or so；用？表示问题 question，如台湾问题可记为：tw？；用&表示和、与，如and, together with；用：表示各种各样"说"的动词 say, speak, talk；用√表示好的、同意，如right, good, agree with等。 S: That's interesting.	
What kind of exercise to write	T: 我们记录下来的信息可以用于选择题，判断题，填空题和回答问题。我们一起来试一试吧！ S: Ok.	多媒体配合方式： PPT第16页 设计意图： 介绍听力题型。
Exercise	T: Tell me your notes. S: You see. Int, info, coun, Jap, fms prgrm. T: Let's check the answers！No1. the Internet. S: No. 2 information. T: No. 3 countries. S: No. 4 Japan. T: No. 5 famous programs. T: 温馨提示，你所记录的信息不要偏离所设题目的大意。 S: 也就是说我们听力前一定要先浏览问题，做到心中有数，对吧？ T: 是的。	多媒体配合方式： PPT第17页。 设计意图： 通过练习进行方法运用。
Summary	T: 本节微课主要讲了如何通过缩略词、数学符号和标点符号进行快速记录，在平时的听力练习中，不妨一试哦！That's all！Thank you.	多媒体配合方式： PPT第18页。 设计意图： 总结本节课的主要内容。

二、听力微技能之细节理解微课设计脚本

1. 基本信息

基本信息

微课名称	听力微技能之细节理解	微课类型	听力微技能
授课/制作人	郑艳霞	制作方式	CS录屏软件+PPT
适用对象	九年级学生	时长	9分钟
教学目标	学习听力微技能之细节理解的具体题型:获取直接信息、判断人物关系、时间判断、数字计算和分析对话场景。		
创新与亮点	举例说明,例子通俗易懂,让学生一看就会。		

2. 设计与录制脚本

设计与录制脚本

教学步骤/活动	教学语言表述内容	多媒体配合方式与设计意图
Greeting & Learning goals	T:欢迎进入东莞市初中英语微课堂。我是清溪中学曾素文。本节微课主要学习听力微技能之细节理解。	多媒体配合方式:PPT第1~2页。设计意图:介绍本节课课题。
Lead-in	T:细节理解题在听力题型中占大部分,因此,了解细节理解题型的分类对提高听力水平有一定帮助。那细节理解具体有哪些呢?它们有获取直接信息、判断任务关系、时间判断、数字计算和分析对话场景。	多媒体配合方式:PPT第3页。设计意图:介绍本节课学习目标。
Process	T:①获取直接信息。这两题的答案都是可以直接从说话者的话语中得知。②判断人物关系。本题考查的是对话者之间的关系,从witness, take notes, sign your names等信息可以判断出话者的关系。③时间判断。时间判断题要注意两点,一是所问的时间,二是对话出现的时间。④数字计算。数字计算题与时间判断题类似,对话中出现的数字题一定要听清,而不是仅听数字本身。⑤分析对话场景。由说话人的客套语气以及a single room等信息可以判断出他们所处的场景。	多媒体配合方式:PPT第4~8页。设计意图:学习听力微技能之细节理解的具体题型。

续 表

教学步骤/活动	教学语言表述内容	多媒体配合方式与设计意图
Exercise	T：最后，我们来完成这道综合题。	多媒体配合方式： PPT 第9页。 设计意图： 学以致用。
Summary	T：回顾一下细节理解的具体类型，它们是获取直接信息、判断人物关系、时间判断、数字计算和分析对话场景。That's all, thank you!	多媒体配合方式： PPT 第10页。 设计意图： 总结巩固。

三、优课课例1：Unit 1 Can you play the guitar？（听说课）

（一）Analysis of Students（学情分析）

Students have learnt about some common instruments（piano, violin, guitar...）and the expressions about abilities（sing, swim, dance, play chess, speak English, play the guitar...）. They can express their likes and dislikes by using I like..., I don't like..., I want to... But students know few about the micro-skills about listening. They love to watch micro-course about students at school. So in this lesson, students will talk about abilities about themselves at school.

（二）Analysis of the Teaching Material（教材分析）

Students have learnt about Yes/No questions and short answers last term. This is the first unit in new term. Students need to talk about their after-school activities at the beginning of each term, so the topic of this lesson is joining a club.

（三）Teaching Goals（教学目标）

1. Target language

Can you swim?

Yes, I can./ No, I can't.

What can you do?

I can dance./I can't sing.

What club do you want to join?

We want to join the chess club.

2. Ability goals

（1）To develop student ability of listening and speaking skills.

（2）To develop student ability of judgment.

（3）To foster student abilities of communication and their innovation.

3. Strategy goals

Task-based approach（任务型教学法），Situational approach（情境教学法）, The communicative language teaching（交际教学法）.

4. Emotional goals

Learn to know what one can do and what one can't do and try to develop one's interests.

5. Teaching aid

A computer for multimedia use.

（Teaching aid： A computer for multimedia use）

Teaching procedures

Procedures	Teacher activities	Student activities	Ways
Lead-in（2 minutes）	Present students some pictures about school activities. Then help students say some of them.	Watch and try to say out the activities in the pictures.	1. 组织课堂，让学生明确本节课的话题。2. 联系旧知，唤醒学生对本话题的元认知。
Pre-listening（10 minutes）	1. Have students look at the pictures in P2 2d and predict what clubs they are talking about.2. Have students watch a video.	Predict, listen, watch and learn.	1. 听力技巧指导：预测。2. 学生观看微视频，学习听力微技能。
While-listening（20 minutes）	1. Have students read through the table and predict what kind of information to listen to.2. Then have students listen and fill in the blanks.3. Check the answer.	Predict, listen and fill in the blanks.	通过听力练习，训练学生预测的听力微技能。

续 表

Procedures	Teacher activities	Student activities	Ways
While-listening（20 minutes）	1. Have students listen to other three passages about activities. 2. Have students reconstruct the three passages. 3. Guide students to complete the self-assessment form.	1. Take notes individually. Work in groups to reconstruct the passages. 2. Discuss together to find out the causes of mistakes. 3. Read the original text aloud.	1. 通过听力练习，训练学生听主旨大意、听细节、推论和选听的听力微技能。 2. 学生通过笔记记录，重组文章并用自己的话表述出来。 3. 学生完成自我评价。
Post-listening（10 minutes）	Have students talk about what they can do in groups by using filler expressions.	Work in groups, share and take notes.	1. 根据听力内容，结合自身实际情况，学生进行小组讨论。 2. 训练学生小组合作学习的能力。
Summary（2 minutes）	Sum up the listening skills.	Review what they have learnt in today's lesson.	复习巩固所学内容。
Homework（1 minutes）	Ask five students about their like and dislike and what they can do and then invite them to join a club together.		口头作业，适当拓展。

（四）Classroom Record（课堂实录）

Step 1：Lead-in

T：Class begins! Good morning, boys and girls!

C：Good morning, teacher!

T：In this lesson, we are going to talk about the activities at school or out of school. Since it is the beginning of this semester, many students hope to learn something else after school, right, for example, playing basketball. By the way, can you play basketball? Can you play basketball well?

（设计意图：根据学生的实际情况引入话题，自然而合理；最后两个问题分层次提问，激发学生的好胜心。）

T：Look at the pictures, can you tell me something about the pictures?

C/S：Play basketball, swim, sing, play chess...

（设计意图：通过话题激发学生的元认知，为本节课作词汇铺垫，并在此活动中加入本节课的新词汇，以旧带新。）

Step 2：Pre-listening

T：Look at the picture, what can you see in this picture?

C/S：A book, a soccer ball, and a pen...

T：So, from the picture, we can predict about the soccer club, the story telling club and the art club, right? This is called prediction. Now let's watch a micro-course about listening skills. After watching the video, please answer the following questions：①How many listening skills does it mention? ②What are they?

（设计意图：通过学习微课，了解五种听力微技能。）

Step 3：While-listening

T：We just knew about five kinds of listening skills. How can we use them? Let's have a try! Look at the sentences, what can you know from the information? Can you predict?

Listen to the conversations and answer the questions.

Check their answers.

（设计意图：通过听力练习，训练学生预测听主旨大意的听力技能。）

T：Look at the table, read through the table, you are going to listen to three conversations, listen and fill in the tables.

Check the answers.

（设计意图：通过听力练习，训练学生听细节、推论和选听的听力技能。）

T：Now, according to the information in the table, tell something about the three students to your partner in your own words. You have one minute to get ready.

（设计意图：通过用自己的语言重组文章，让学生进一步熟悉听力材料，并学会灵活运用目标句型。）

The whole class read the original material together.

（设计意图：通过朗读听力原材料，学生可以与自己重组的文章进行对比，进行评价。）

Guide the students to complete the self-assessment form.

Step 4：Post-listening

T：Work in groups of four, talk about what you can do and what club you can join. Take notes while your teammates are talking, after your group-work, share your information in the class.

（设计意图：小组合作进行对话，让学生巩固运用目标语言，训练学生记笔记的技能。）

Step 5：Summary

T：Now let's review what we have learned today. What kinds of listening skills do you know?

（设计意图：教师和学生的最后总结让学生对自己今天学习的知识进行了梳理，又一次强化，加深印象。）

Step 6：Homework

Ask five students about their like and dislike and what they can do and then invite them to join a club together.

（设计意图：布置口头作业，增加学生课后练习听说的机会。）

（五）Teaching Reflection（教学反思）

1. 本课是对听力技能微视频教学的尝试与摸索

本节听力课通过听前活动观看微视频，学习听力微技能。在听力教学中，我在选材上做了一定的尝试，主要考虑了以下几个方面：材料具有真实性、交际性；材料中的语速属于自然语速；材料提供能让学生感兴趣和能激发学生学习动机的语境。因此，在根据本课主题确定话题后，我在网上收集了相关信息并对材料做了修改，在修改过程中着重结合学生的认知水平去控制材料的难度。课后回收自我评估表共46份，在第一项：The listening text was _____.
A. very easy B. quite easy C. quite difficult D. impossible（Harris, 1997）中，共有7人选择A，占总人数的15%；36人选择B，占总人数的78%；选择C的仅有3人。从学生所填写的自我评估表来看，材料总体难易适中。

听后自我评估表的使用加强了对学生元认知策略的培养。我在听后采用了Harris的听后评估表，旨在发展学生在听力过程中的自我监控、自我调整以及检验学习效果和效率的能力，促进学生自我反思和自我提升。在此课设计上，由于我加入了Dictogloss（语法听写）的任务，该任务需要小组合作完成，因此我在评价量表上增加了一项：I can do better with / without the help of my group mates,以激发学生思考同伴互助的重要性。从学生所填写的评估表来看，78%的学生认为有了同伴的互助，他们可以更好地完成任务。

2. 要重视对不同层次学生在听力微技能上的指导

在教学预设上，应重视教学难点和重点，突出各环节的针对性。本课的重点是学生通过听对话，巩固和提升听力微技能，特别是在根据已有线索进行预测的微技能方面的训练仍需细化，以便学困生能很好地完成课本上的练习。此外，在记录的过程中，应指导学生使用符号记录，然后再修正。

四、优课课例2：Go For It 八年级上册Unit 1 Where did you go on vacation?

（一）Analysis of Students（学情分析）

Students are interested in the topic about holidays and vacations because they can talk about what they like, they can share their experience with others, they have something to talk about, which is the most important. So, generally speaking, they will be active and cooperate well with each other .

（二）Analysis of the Teaching Material（教材分析）

This lesson is about past events about holidays and vacations. Students will talk about where they went, when they went, who they went with, how they went, what they did and how they felt.

（三）Teaching Goals（教学目标）

1. Target language

Where did you go on vacation?

I went to New York City.

Did you go out with anyone?

No. No one was here. Everyone was on vacation.

How was the food?

Everything tasted really good!

2. Ability goals

（1）To develop student ability of listening and speaking skills.

（2）Learn to share experience by talking about past events.

（3）To foster student abilities of communication and their innovation.

3. Strategy goals

Task-based approach（任务型教学法）, Situational approach（情境教学法）, The communicative language teaching（交际教学法）.

4. Emotional goals

Learn to know about how to travel politely.

5. Teaching aid

A computer for multimedia use.

（Teaching aid： A computer for multimedia use）

Teaching procedures

Steps	Teacher activities	Student activities	Ways
Step 1： Lead-in	Play a video about traveling in different places.	Watch the video and enjoy the beautiful scenery.	课前预热，提示学生本节课的话题。
	Show students pictures.	Say out the places or activities.	通过图片检测学生原有词汇。
	Ask students questions.	Answer the questions.	通过问答，激发学生的兴趣。
Step 2： Presentation	Organize students to complete the mind-map.	Complete the mind-map.	通过思维导图，巩固旧词汇，引出新词汇。
Step 3： Micro-course	Play a video about listening skill.	Watch the video and take notes.	通过微视频学习听力微技能：细节理解。
Step 4： Listening practice	Play the tape of material 1.	Listen and choose.	通过听力练习，训练获取直接信息的微技能。
	Play the tape of material 2.	Listen and answer the questions.	通过听力练习，训练判断人物关系的微技能。
	Play the tape of material 3.	Listen and choose.	通过听力练习，训练判断时间的微技能。
	Play the tape of material 4.	Listen and fill in the blank.	通过听力练习，训练数字计算的微技能。

续表

Steps	Teacher activities	Student activities	Ways
Step 4: Listening practice	Play the tape of material 5.	Listen and choose.	通过听力练习，训练分析对话场景的微技能。
	Play the tape of material 6.	Listen and fill in the blank.	通过听力练习，进行以上微技能的综合训练。
Step 5: Group-work	Guide the students to discuss the experience or stories in group.	Discuss the experience or stories in group and take notes.	通过小组讨论，运用目标语言。
Step 6: Sharing	Ask students to give report.	Share their discussion.	通过分享，评价自己的活动。
Step 7: Summary	Sum up the listening skills and the target language.	Review what they have learnt in today's lesson.	通过回忆，复习巩固所学知识。
Step 8: Homework	Ask five students about their experience and find the same thing.		布置口头作业，适当进行拓展。

（四）Classroom Record（课堂实录）

Step 1: Lead-in

T: Let's watch a video and enjoy the beautiful scenery. After watching, please tell me how many places there are in the video.

（设计意图：通过观看视频，让学生集中注意力，引入本节课的话题。）

T: Look at the picture, where is it? / what are they doing?

C/S: …

（设计意图：通过图片问答，了解学生的元认知，唤醒他们的词汇记忆。）

T: Have you been to these places? What did you do on summer vacation?

C/S: …

（设计意图：通过问答，引入本节课的目标语言，引起学生对曾经的旅行的回忆和共鸣。）

Step 2: Presentation

T: Where did you go on vacation? What did you do? Finish the mind-map.（如下图所示）

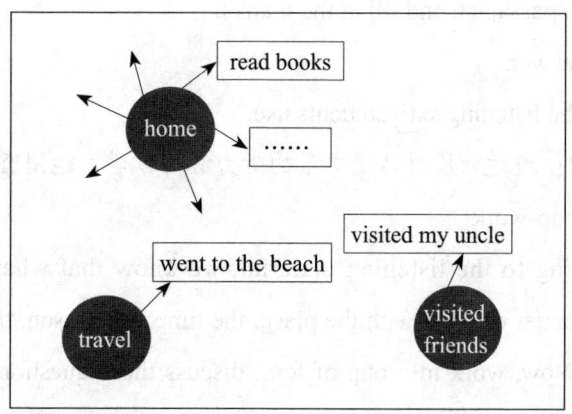

（设计意图：通过补充思维导图，复习旧词汇，学习新词汇。）

Step 3：Micro-course

T：Let's watch a micro-course and take notes.

（设计意图：通过观看微视频，学习了解听力微技能：细节理解。）

Step 4：Listening

T：Listen to passage 1 and choose the right answers.

Check the answer.

Talk about the listening skill students use.

T：Listen to passage 2 and answer the questions.

Check the answer.

Talk about the listening skill students use.

T：Listen to passage 3 and choose the right answers.

Check the answer.

Talk about the listening skill students use.

T：Listen to passage 4 and fill in the blanks.

Check the answer.

Talk about the listening skill students use.

T：Listen to passage 5 and choose the right answer.

Check the answer.

Talk about the listening skill students use.

T: Listen to passage 6 and fill in the blanks.

Check the answer.

Talk about the listening skill students use.

（设计意图：通过六段对话或文章的听力练习，学习运用听力微技能。）

Step 5：Group-work

T: According to the listening material, we know that when we talk about travelling, we'd better connect with the place, the time, the person, the way, the thing and the feeling. Now, work in group of four, discuss these questions together. After the discussion, choose one student from your group to give a report in the class.

（设计意图：通过小组讨论，运用目标语言。）

Step 6：Sharing

T: Now it's time to share you experience.

（设计意图：通过分享经历，学生进行评价和自我评价。）

Step 7：Summary

T: Now let's review what we have learned today. What listening skill do you know?

（设计意图：教师和学生的最后总结让学生对自己今天学习的知识进行了梳理，又一次进行了强化，加深了印象。）

Step 8：Homework

Ask five students about their experience and find the same thing.

（设计意图：通过布置口头作业，增加学生课后练习听说的机会。）

（五）Teaching Reflection（教学反思）

本节课的优点在于把听力微技能融入听说课堂中，并且以谈论旅游为主线贯穿整节课，六个听力材料全部来源于地道的美/英式英语，不同场景的对话，而且都与旅游话题有关，这样除了训练学生的听力微技能之外，还让学生尽可能多地接触不同场景、不同语音语调的说话方式。这些设计能很好地引起学生的兴趣，打破一贯的课堂形式，唯一的不足之处是，各个教学环节的衔接不够紧密。

第三章

阅读技能的微视频设计与实施

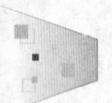
玩转英语课堂的微视频
——初中英语课堂微视频的设计与实施

基于阅读学情的初中英语微视频设计

为了更好地推进我校的课题研究《初中英语微视频的设计与实施》，我接受了一项教研任务，上一节用微视频辅助教学的中考备考阅读公开课，教学内容是：①帮助学生掌握主旨大意题的解题技巧；②以微视频作为辅助教学手段。教学目标是：①通过教授阅读策略之跳读，使学生掌握主旨题的解题方法；②通过学习分析文章结构，按结构提取主旨大意；③通过对比四个选项的设置形式，提高主旨题的得分率。

一、阅读材料分析

中考英语阅读理解主要考查考生在单位时间内快速阅读英语短文，了解短文的主题思想，对文中的信息进行分析、推理或者判断，并把握上下文事实、细节之间的时空顺序和逻辑关系，理解作者的意图、态度以及文章的寓意的能力。纵观近五年的中考阅读题，总共3篇，分A、B、C篇。阅读理解共15小题，每小题2分，总分为30分，占试卷总分（120分）的25%，是整张试卷分值所占比重最大的题目。题型包括细节理解题、推理判断题、词义猜测题和主旨大意题。其中，主旨大意题的难度较大，也是考生感到最为棘手、最容易出错的题。主旨大意题要求学生具有很强的语篇把握能力和分析能力，能够从全局的角度对文章括以总领，梳清脉络。可以说，对阅读理解主旨题的把握能力决定了阅读这个整体题项的成败，它也是衡量学生阅读水平高低的一个重要标尺，所以，如果我们在这道题上能够取得突破，就等于攻克了阅读中最顽固的堡垒。

（一）五年考情（如下表）

五年考情

	2010年	2011年	2012年	2013年	2014年
篇目	B篇	B篇	B篇	B篇	B篇
题数	1道	1道	1道	1道	1道
题号	第65题	第65题	第65题	第65题	第65题
考查内容	概括大意	最佳标题	最佳标题	概括大意	概括大意
主题句的位置	在开头	在结尾	无主题句	无主题句	无主题句
体裁	说明文	说明文	说明文	说明文	说明文
总分值	2分	2分	2分	2分	2分

从上表可以看出，2010—2014年，B篇阅读以说明文为主，说明文旨在说明或解释事物的性质、特征和内在联系。主旨大意题通常在B篇阅读的第65题出现，考查的范围主要有寻找最佳标题和概括文章大意。

（二）命题方式

主旨大意题主要针对文章的主题、中心思想、文章的结构层次（主题句或主题段），要求学生在理解全文后归纳文章要点。它主要有以下两类题干表现形式。

1. 概括文章中心思想或段落大意的题干

The main idea for the passage is _____.（2010年，第65题）

What is the main idea of this passage? （2013年，第65题）

The passage is mainly about _____.（2014年，第65题）

2. 选择标题的题干

Which is the best title of the passage? （2011 年，第65题）

What is the best title of the passage? （2012年，第65题）

二、学情分析

根据我对所教班级的观察与调查，发现学生们普遍都害怕做主旨大意题，觉得"老做老错"，虽然看得懂文章，句子的结构也很清楚，考试时还看了又看，看了两三遍了，但到最后还是选错了答案。那么，做主旨题时，学生们常犯什么错误？这些错误应怎样避免呢？经过研究，发现同学们做主旨题最常犯的错误是"无视主题，以点带面"，也就是在阅读时，未能把握文章的主题或忽视了主题；做题时，只知其一，不知其二，未能掌握干扰项的特点。

干扰项主要有以下三个特点。

1. 无中生有

有些选项单独看是正确的，但在短文中没有提到或有的选项中的某些词语取自文章中，但经过推敲之后你会发现这类选项的内容与文章的内容不相符。

2. 以偏概全

有些选项只阐述了文章的部分内容，这往往会让学生在选择答案时举棋不定。

3. 概括不够或概括过度

错误选项归纳的主题以部分代整体，或超出了文章实际所涉及的内容，缺乏针对性。

例如，2014年广东省中考试题第65题。

65. This passage is mainly about _____.

  A. the sales of the umbrella

  B. the differences among umbrellas

  C. the invention of the umbrella

  D. the history and the use of the umbrella

选项A"雨伞的销售"，文章没提及，与主题毫无关系，属无中生有。选项C"雨伞的发明"是文章中的一个点，属于以偏概全。选项B"雨伞的不同之处"超出了文章所涉及的内容。只有选项D"雨伞的历史与作用"才是正确答案。

三、微视频的设计

要在阅读课中插入微视频，那么微视频插在教学过程的哪个步骤好呢？本微视频的亮点是什么？怎样使学生看完了微视频后，觉得有所收获，并且兴趣盎然地想继续阅读？

根据考纲要求和学生实际，把本微视频的学习目标设为通过跳读获取文章大意，把视频的流程设计为"三个步骤""三个特点""三种技巧"。

（一）三个步骤

1. skimming 跳读

做主旨大意题常用的方法是"跳读法"（skimming）。它是一种快速浏览的阅读方式，力求在尽可能短的时间里理解文章的大意，任务单一，目标集中，可以略读文章的标题，通过文章的首尾段以及每段的首尾句来判断、预测主要内容，了解文章大意。

2. 找主题句

文章的主旨是通过段落来表达的，而段落大意主要由主题句来体现，因为主题句表达中心思想，其他句子均围绕主题句进行展开，因此识别各段落的主题句并由此归纳出文章的中心思想是解答该类题的关键，所以做主旨大意题最有效的方法是通读短文，找出文中的主题句。主题句一般出现在段首、段尾或段中。

（1）主题句在段首。

例如，Smoking cigarettes is harmful to your health. Experiments show that cigarette smoking can cause cancer. Besides the most serious and terrible disease （illness）, cancer, cigarette smoking also can cause other health problems. For example, it can give one a "smoker's cough". Finally, studies have shown it is easy for cigarette smokers to catch colds. Whether you get an unimportant cold or terrible killer, cancer, smoking is harmful. Is it worth it? （1.5分钟）

65. What is the passage mainly about?

  A. Smoking can cause cancer.

  B. Smoking is a terrible killer.

  C. Smoking is harmful to our health.

  D. An experiment on smoking.

一个主题句常常是一个段落的开头，其后的句子则是论证性细节。正确答案为：C。

（2）主题句在段尾。

例如，If you buy some well-made clothes, you can save money because they can last longer. They look good even after they have been washed many times.

Sometimes some clothes cost more money, but it does not mean that they always better made, or they always fit better. In other words, some less expensive clothes look and fit better than the more expensive clothes.

  65. The main idea for the passage is＿＿＿＿.

    A. buying less expensive clothes

    B. washing clothes in a right way

    C. being a clever clothes shopper

    D. choosing the well-made clothes

用归纳法写文章时，往往表述细节的句子在前，概述性的句子在后，并以此结尾。这种位于段末或篇末的主题句往往是对前面细节的总结、归纳或结论。正确答案为：C。

（3）没有主题句怎么办？

有时，一篇文章里没有明显的主题句，这时我们应该怎样确定文章的主题或中心思想呢？其实这也不难。①搞清楚是问某一段还是全文的大意，可利用文中的主要信息来把握文脉，进行综合归纳，概括文章的主题；②若有标题，标题中蕴含的信息往往是关键信息；③任何一篇文章都是围绕某个主题展开的，因此，许多文章中最明显的特点之一是有一个反复出现的中心词，即高频词，也叫作主题词。抓住它，便抓住了文章的中心。

例如，In February 2013, the State Council（国务院）encouraged primary and high schools to give students a spring and autumn break without changing the total number of student vocation days.

What do they think of the new breaks?

Some students think spring and autumn breaks would give them more time to relax and play outdoors. Others worry that the new breaks would mean more homework. "As soon as we finish our holiday homework, the new term will begin." Qi Kai, a six-grade boy in Beijing told Yangtze Evening News. "It seems there would be no time for us to play."

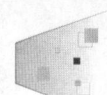

续表

	Teachers are worried about the idea. Some are concerned that the new breaks would affect students 'study. "In the first one or two weeks before and after holidays, students are very excited. Teachers have to make them concentrate on students." Xu Lei,an English teacher,told China Daily.
	Many parents are not happy with the idea.They have to help there kids make holiday plans.What's more,the added breaks will mean short summer and winter holidays. "This will make it difficult to plan long trips." Wang Li,the mother of an 8-year-old primary school student,told China Daily.

65. The passage mainly tells us _____.

    A. teachers welcome the breaks

    B. parents and students hope to have more breaks

    C. people have different opinion about the new breaks

    D. students can have less homework during the breaks

这篇文章没有主题句，遇到这种情况，应如何通过关键词来概括呢？找关键词，首先要找出题干与选项的关键词，然后找到文章中的关键词。如上文，四个选项中都有一个breaks,而且new break 在文章中多次出现，它是文章的高频词或中心词，所以本文是围绕着"What do you think of the new break？"而展开的。选项A 、B、 D 中的teachers，parents and students只是文章中的细节，所以答案为：C。

3. 确定答案

选取与作者在文章中要表达的意思最吻合的选项，明确具体答案。

（二）三大特点

为了让学生尽快掌握主旨大意题的解题方法，要把主旨题的特点浓缩为三个字"精、准、全"：①精——语言精练，短小精悍；②准——能准确地表达作者的观点；③全——涵盖性强，能覆盖全文。具体地说，就是用精练的语言概括出文章的中心思想，注意文章的内涵和外延，把作者的观点准确地表达出来。另外，要排除那些片面的选项，选择包含文章的主要内容及作者观点的选项，范围不宜过大或过小。

（三）三种技巧

做好主旨题，除了找出主题句之外，还要区分选项之间的细微差别，仔细剔除干扰项。命题者在出这类题时，常常利用生活常识编出干扰项，把文中的细节当主旨，利用局部信息编造干扰项，编制超过文章范围的标题或不能涵盖文章中心意义的标题来考查考生的理解程度，同学们要特别留意。做这类题目时，先采取排除法，缩小范围后，再联系上下文，排除片面的选项，选择最具概况性或总结性的答案。为了让学生能尽快区分干扰项，把主旨大意题的解题技巧编成了口诀：一找，二比，三定，即①找主题句或高频词；②论字排辈，比比"谁大谁小"；③确定答案。

（四）声音的制作

好听的声音是微视频的"生命之水"，所以本次微视频的录制，需要用专用录微视频的microphone，在录制前打好稿件，以减少在录音时的口误。另外，为了使视频令人兴奋一些，教师要同时扮演两个角色：教师与学生，语调多变，还加入一些幽默元素。例如，没有主题句怎么办？我这样解说："老师，你让我们找主题句，但我们看了好几遍了，都没找到主题句，这可怎么办呀？Help？""是的，文章如果没有主题句，这可怎么办呢？""不用怕，不必慌！老师有好点子，本文中有一个词反复出现了好多次，你看到了吗？睁大你的眼睛，找到了没？Bingo,you are clever. It is new break.当文中找不到主题句时，我们可以找它的高频词或中心词。"又如，在解说做主旨题的解题技巧"比一比，比'谁大谁小'时，要这样解说："比——论字排辈，比比'谁大谁小'，小的要服从大的，通过比较排位，看看谁是文章中的'老大'。"通过这样生动形象的语言，学生都觉得特别有趣，听得特别认真。

四、教学实例分析与展示

（一）Lead in（导入）

向学生展示2015年广东省学生毕业水平考试英语试卷的结构，让学生猜测试卷里第四大题是什么、题量多少、分值如何、中考阅读理解题有哪几种常见的题型、你觉得哪道题难度最大。

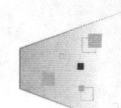

简单直接的导入，让学生的注意力马上集中到阅读的重要性上，也引出了当堂课的主题——主旨题的解题技巧。接着，又提出了两个问题：①你知道主旨题的特点吗？②做主旨题需要哪些技巧？然后让学生观看自录的微视频。看完后，让学生复述主旨题的特点与技巧。最后，让学生们做近五年的中考题，考查他们是否掌握了主旨题的解题方法。

（二）Skimming（跳读）

Task 1：Think！Think！Think！

2012年的B篇是介绍Barbie，考虑到学生对 Barbie既熟悉，又喜欢，所以决定用Barbie 作为切入点。在课堂上用了一个会说话的Barbie 去引入有关的背景知识，用mind-map的形式跟学生讨论Barbie：①Do you know full name of Barbie? ②Where does she come from? ③How old is Barbie? ④ In China,which city did Barbie visit first? Mattle opened its first Barbie shop store in Shanghai in 2009. As you see, Barbie has been in China for 6 years.Now Barbie can speak Chinese. And Barbie has a Chinese name, too. Do you want to know it? 通过实物的引入，学生跟Barbie的距离拉近了，也很好奇Barbie的中文名是什么。接着，再让Barbie自己介绍自己，学生们热情高涨。同学们，你们想更多地了解Barbie吗？请阅读2012年的B篇，然后告诉老师："What is the best title of the passage？"

（2012年·广东省）B篇

Fifty-three years ago Barbie Millicent Roberts first appeared in the world of toys. Since then, Barbie doll，as everyone called her，has become the most successful toy doll in history. Her parent, the Mattel Company，said that 90% of all American girls between 3 and 10 have at least one Barbie at home.

However，Barbie is facing some trouble at present（现在）. There are many similar dolls on the market in competition with her. Another doll named Bratz, for example, came to life thirteen years ago. She looks more like today's pop stars with heavy makeup（浓妆）and miniskirts. And her company offers more kinds of clothes too.

It seems that Barbie has lost her magic among older girls． "For younger girls, playing with a Barbie is much fun. But when you get older, you want something smarter and more modern, " says Vera Shepherd, a shop assistant in a New York toy store.

It is good news that on the international market, Barbie is still No.1. Although Mattel is selling fewer Barbies in the United States these years, sales in other countries are still going up. In January 2009, Mattel opened its first Barbie store in Shanghai, where girls can shop, eat, drink or even become <u>fashion designers</u> for their own Barbies.

Mattel is planning big celebrations for Barbie's 53rd birthday. Fashion designers from all over the world have been called to make new dresses for Barbie. How long will Barbie stay popular in the world of toy dolls? It is hard to say, but 53 is surely not the age to retire （退休）.

（　　）65. What is the best title of the passage?

　　A. First Barbie Shop in Shanghai

　　B. Barbie's Past and Present

　　C. Barbie's 53rd Birthday Party

　　D. Barbie Lost Her Magic

本题各个选项分析如下图所示：

Barbie 的文章分为五段，每段的第一句是该段的主题句，而且文章有明显的时间线索，考生只要把各段的主题句归纳起来就可以知道该文章的大意。

第三章 阅读技能的微视频设计与实施

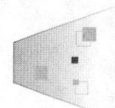

Task 2：Practice makes perfect

2014年的B篇阅读是关于umbrella的。它与2012年的B篇Barbie结构一样，因此，它们的解题方法相似。

（2014年·广东省）B篇

To us, it seems so natural to put up an umbrella to keep the water off when it rains. But in fact the umbrella was not invented as protection against the rain. Its first use was as a shade（遮蔽）against the sun.

Nobody knows who first invented it, but the umbrella was used in very ancient times. Probably the first to use it were the Chinese, back in the eleventh century BC.

We know that the umbrella was used in ancient Egypt and Babylon as a sunshade. And there was a strange thing connected with its use： it became a symbol of honor and power（权力）. In the Far East in ancient times, the umbrella was allowed to be used only by those in high office or by royal people such as the kings or queens.

In Europe, the Greeks were the first to use the umbrella as a sunshade. The umbrella was in common use in ancient Greece, but it is believed that the first people in Europe to use the umbrella as protection against the rain were the ancient Romans. During the middle ages in Europe, the use of the umbrella almost disappeared. Then it appeared again in Italy in the late sixteenth century. And again it became a symbol of power.

Umbrellas have not changed much in style during all this time, though they have become much lighter in weight. It wasn't until the twentieth century that the umbrellas for women began to be made in all kinds of colors.

65. This passage is mainly about _____.

    A. the sales of the umbrella

    B. the differences among umbrellas

    C. the invention of the umbrella

    D. the history and the use of the umbrella

文章分为五段：第一段：the use of the umbrella；第二段：the history of the umbrella；第三段：the use of the umbrella；第四段：the use of the umbrella；第五

段：the history of the umbrella. 把五段大意整合在一起，可以推断答案为：D. the history and the use of the umbrella.

Task 3: Find! Find! Find!

（2013年·广东省）B篇

In nature, you may see many insects（昆虫）and animals of different colors. Have you ever wondered why?

Locusts are super delicious food for birds, but it is not always an easy job for birds to catch them. It is neither because locusts are good jumpers or runners nor because they are smarter than their enemies. The reason is that the colors of locusts change with the colors of crops（庄稼）. When crops are young, locusts look green. But when autumn comes, locusts change to the yellow and brown color as crops do.

Brown bears, tigers and other animals move quietly through forests. They can't be seen easily by their enemies. This is because they have colors similar to the trees. For the same reason, polar bears that live on a land of snow and ice are white. Butterflies and bees living among the flowers are colorful like flowers. Soil insects are mostly dark-colored and they live under the soil（土壤）in a dark and wet environment. However, insects with colors different from plants can easily be found and eaten by others. So in order to survive, they have to hide themselves in the daytime and appear only at night.

Have you ever noticed some even stranger acts? The ink fish in the sea can send out some very black ink when it faces danger. As the ink spreads over, its enemies will find themselves suddenly in a dark world. At the same time the ink fish immediately swims away. That is how it keeps itself safe though it is not strong at all.

65. What is the main ides of this passage?

  A. Some insects and animals have different skills.

  B. Some insects and animals are clever than we think.

  C. Some insects and animals use colors to protect themselves.

  D. Some insects and animals can get used to the environment easily.

2013中考题的B篇中没有主题句，但有一个反复出现的高频词：color。选项A与选项B只是文章的细节信息，答案D"一些昆虫和动物很容易适应环境"属于生活常识，不能用生活常识代替全文的主题，故答案为：C。

Task 4：Consolidation

（2015年·广东中考模拟）B篇

Different countries and different people have different manners.We must find out their customs so that they will not think us impolite.Here are examples of the things that a person with good education does or does not do.

If you visit a Chinese family, you should knock at the door first.When the door opens,you will not move before the host says "Come in, please." After you enter the room,you would not sit down until the host asks you to take a seat.When a cup of tea is put on a tea table before you or sent to your hand,you will say "Thank you" and receive it with two hands,not one hand,or they will think you have ill manners .Before entering a house in Japan,it is a good manner to take off your shoes.In European countries,even though shoes sometimes become very dirty,this is not done.In a Malay （马来人的） house,a visitor never finishes the food on the table.He leaves a little to show that he has had enough.In England,a visitor always finished a drink or the food to show that he has enjoyed it.This will make the host pleased.

5. Which is the best title of the passage?

   A. Manners in Different Countries

   B. People in Different Countries

   C. Foods in Different Countries

   D. Manners in Different Countries

文章的开头句：Different countries and different people have different manners.

技巧点拨：注意开头句、结尾句、高频词。可以推断文章的标题为"Manners in Different Countries"，故答案为：D。

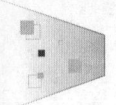

五、课后反思

第一，本堂课运用了微视频作为辅助手段，基于学生的认知规律，注意学生的阅读策略——跳读的培养，使学生在体验中学习，掌握主旨题的特点与解题技巧，体现了新课改精神。

第二，通过口诀、技巧点拨，使学生快速掌握主旨题的解题技巧，大部分学生都沉浸在课堂教学中。

然而，有少数学生英语基础较差，词汇量有限，他们不能有效地完成阅读任务。作为一位中学教师，我应该如何提高学生的英语阅读能力呢？我感到任重而道远，为此，在日后的教学中仍需不断完善教学方法，从而提高初中英语阅读复习课的有效性和高效性。

初中英语阅读微视频教学的具体实施

一、问题的提出

"读书使人进步"。古今中外,读书对人的塑造和重要性深入人心。初中英语阅读作为学生提高英语学科核心素养的关键环节,肩负着保证学生学习效果、拓展学生阅读视野、建构和谐立德树人的重任。但是,如果只依靠教材,仅限于英语课堂内的阅读是无法完成此重任的,通过大量的课外阅读,学生的人文素养和核心素养才能不断提高,起到阅读本身对人的塑造作用。《义务教育英语课程标准》(2011年版)(以下称《课程标准》)对初中英语阅读教学提出了具体的要求:"文化知识的教学应以促进学生文化意识的形成和发展为目标。文化学习不仅需要知识的积累,还需要深入理解其精神内涵,并将优秀文化进一步内化为个人的意识和品行。"同时指出,"除了课堂和教材所包括的语篇外,需要特别指出的是,广泛阅读可以让学生体验更丰富的语篇文体,如对话、小说、传记、新闻报道和报刊文章、网络媒体的代表性文章等语篇类型,使他们逐步养成良好的阅读习惯,通过阅读发展阅读能力,通过阅读学习语言和人文、科学知识,通过阅读拓展思维,提高审美、鉴赏和评价的能力"。目前,初中英语课内外阅读衔接不畅,彼此分隔,课内阅读偏重应试、只重技巧,课外阅读无法保证、不受重视。这样的现状造成了学生无法"得法于课内,得益于课外",以至于学生的英语核心素养提升缓慢。因此,探索如何在有限的课外阅读教学时间里精准定位,进行精准教学,培养学生的文化意识,提升学生英语核心素养的研究成了一个热点话题。

二、理论基础

网络的迅猛发展在对传统的教育理念和教育模式产生巨大冲击的同时，也为现代信息技术背景下教学模式和学习方式的变革提供了丰富的课程资源。微视频就以其特有的优点被广泛地运用于教学中。

在国外，最早把微视频运用于英语阅读教学的是美国新墨西哥州圣胡安学院的高级教学设计师、学院在线服务经理David Penrose。2008年，他提出了建设微视频教程的五个步骤：罗列教学核心概念；为核心概念提供上下文背景；录制长为1~3分钟的视频；引导学生阅读或探索课程知识的课后任务；将教学视频和课程任务上传到课程管理系统。

国内学者认为将微视频运用于初中英语阅读教学，可以将阅读文本中抽象的生词、陌生的场景、远离学生生活的话题等幻化为有声有形、多维的形象展现，有助于学生理解阅读材料。陆燕峰研究了如何将微视频运用于初中英语阅读教学中，他通过实践研究后指出，在英语教学中应用微视频时，微视频的选择很重要，要选择那些比较贴近学生生活、学生比较容易理解的场景，这样才能够更好地创设相应的情境。王觅指出，运用微视频可以帮学生对阅读材料进行很好的建构。可见，运用微视频辅助英语阅读教学，可以提高学生的英语阅读理解水平。但是运用微视频在英语课外阅读教学中培养学生文化意识的研究在国内还不多见，本文正是探讨如何在有限的英语课外阅读教学中，合理巧妙地运用微视频，精准教学，更好地帮助学生感知、理解、分析、讨论阅读材料即语篇所承载的文化内涵和价值取向，帮助学生理解更深层次的意义内涵，起到画龙点睛的作用，助力培养学生的文化意识，形成自己的人文核心素养。

传统观点认为从文章中获取信息，了解文章的内容就达到了阅读的目的。现在语言学家提出了新的看法："阅读是一个语言心理的猜测过程。"读者在对语篇层次的词语进行解码的同时，也在运用自己的知识（包括社会文化方面的知识、有关阅读材料话题的知识、文章结构组织的知识、情景上下文的知识等）对文章的下文进行预测，阅读检验自己的预测、修订自己的预测、进行新的预测……整个阅读过程实际上就是读者与文章的交互过程。只有低层次阅读和高层次阅读共同作用，才能实现流利阅读的目的。这样的阅读才能激发学生的思维、想象和创造能力，而这也正是阅读教学的目的。《课程标准》也指出"文化知识的教学"："这是一个内化于心、外化于行的过程，涉及几个步骤的演进和融合：感知中外文化知识——分析与比较；认同优秀文化——赏析与汲取；加深文化理解——认知与内化；形成文明素养——行为与表征。"

在英语阅读教学中，微视频提供的真实的情景，能够很好地帮助学生理解课文内容和文化差异，韩秀荣指出，从选题上看，微视频通常以表现某个知识点，或表现某个动作技能及操作的演示过程为主要特征；从内容上看，它以记录型的素材、资料为主，也可以是编境，通过提供思维素材，实施趣味评价，丰富教学形式，优化教学过程，创造精彩的英语课堂，能够加速学生的感知过程和促进认知深化，最大限度地挖掘学生的创新精神，从而使学生乐学、爱学英语。

三、培养学生文化意识的实践

运用微视频，在初中英语课外阅读教学中培养学生文化意识的实践，通过对《课程标准》关于课外阅读教学提示的解读，可以发现，微视频短小精悍，集声音、文字、动画等于一体的形式，能够为学生提供更加真实的情境，让学生有身临其境的感觉，既能激发学生学习英语的兴趣和积极性，更可以通过精准地选择微视频，有意识地引入阅读的重点，为教学重点、难点的精准突破设下伏笔。

（一）运用微视频，加强跨文化交流

结合教材内容，运用微视频开展听读活动，有意识地帮助学生了解英美等国家主要传统节日，比较中外传统节日的异同，探讨文化认同、文化传承的价值和意义；拓宽国际视野，理解和包容不同文化，进而提高跨文化交际能力。

以人教版（2011）新目标（Go for it！）八年级上"Unit10 If you go to the party, you will have a great time！"为例。通过研读该单元的Section A所设计的各个环节，可以观察出它们都围绕着一个主题——Party。文化背景知识的教学可以是了解西方的"派对"文化。在对整个主题单元的教学设计中的最后一部分，设置收集问题环节：西方最流行的"Halloween（万圣节）"马上要到了，你知道是什么时候吗？你对"万圣节"有哪些疑问呢？

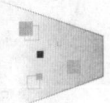
玩转英语课堂的微视频
——初中英语课堂微视频的设计与实施

根据教科书的安排，可以结合时间在万圣节前讨论这个话题。选择万圣节的原因：一是了解世界上主要的节假日及庆祝方式是《课程标准》文化意识五级目标的其中一项；二是近年来万圣节在中国年轻群体中很流行，这一话题能迅速引起学生的学习欲望；三是关于万圣节的争议不断。一些不了解西方文化的人反感万圣节的最大原因是对"鬼"这个概念的理解不同。这正是《课程标准》里提到的"提高对中外文化异同敏感性和鉴别能力，尊重和包容文化的多样性，进而提高跨文化交际能力"。根据学生课堂上的掌握情况和收集的问题，设计一个课后听读的文化微视频，对学生进行精准分层阅读教学，课堂形式实现了由教师主导的课堂向学生学习的课堂转变。

微视频的设计简案如下表所示。

万圣节文化专题微视频设计简案

概况	主题	万圣节简介
	教学目标	了解西方万圣节的常识
	学习对象	八年级学生
	整体时长	5分钟
内容设计	教学环节	导入：以万圣节标志物的图片和声效引出主题
		中间：1. 万圣节的起源和发展。 2. 万圣节的象征物。 3. 万圣节的活动。
		结尾：中西方文化差异：对"鬼"的态度
制作	所需工具	电脑（Windows XP以上系统）
	制作软件	CS软件，PPT软件，绘声绘影软件
	录制方式	录屏式
	视频格式	MP4

（二）运用微视频，汲取优秀精神营养

运用微视频编写阅读材料，有意识地帮助学生理解和欣赏寓言，感悟其蕴涵的精神，汲取其中的优秀营养，获得积极的人生态度和价值观念。

本课例是我市某实验中学一位老师的公开研讨课例，是基于翻转课堂的课外阅读教学专题课。课前，教师播放了一个寓言故事的微视频给学生观看：一

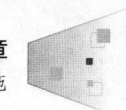

位勤劳工作的葡萄园主在临死前让自己两个懒惰的儿子去寻找葡萄园的宝藏，两个儿子在努力找寻的过程中，悟出了勤劳付出是真正的宝藏的道理。教师根据这个微视频，编写了以下的英语课外阅读材料，并设计了基于该语篇主题的导学案和教学活动流程。

1. 编写阅读材料

根据微视频编写的阅读材料如下所示。

The Treasure in the Vineyard

There once lived a grade grower with a big vineyard.This grade grower has too lazy sons. "Boys,come and help！Then you can learn how to care for the grapes！"

"Dad,you're better at it,so you do it.We are going to hang out with our friends." Although the father was eager to teach the boys,they were never interested in learning.

One day,the farmer had a serious illness.So he called for his sons to leave his last words. "I hid the treasure in our vineyard for the two of you.When I'm gone,make sure you look for it together！" After he died,the two sons went out to search for the treasure but it was not easy to find the treasure that was buried in the vineyard. "How are we going to find the treasure here？" They continue to dig day and night. However,there was still no treasure.

Time passed and autumn arrived. "Wow！Come here and look at there plump grapes.Have you ever seen such big and juicy-looking grapes before？" one of them asked. "No,never！They are as sweet as honey,too." The other repiled.The two sons jumped with excitement and said, "this is the treasure father was talking about！"

"You are right！He was trying to show us how to enjoy the fruits of our hard work." the elder brother said.

From that day on,the brother understood the rewards of hard work and they continued to work hard every day.Their father was watching them from the heaven and he was happy to see his sons finally working together.

2. 设计教学流程图

这节翻转课堂的教学活动流程图设计如下图所示。

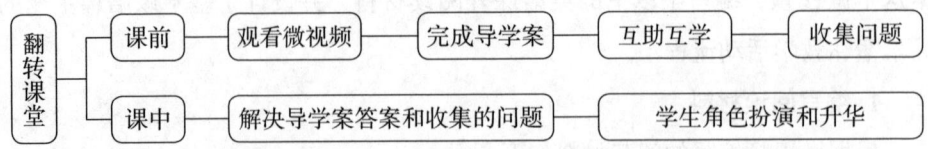

3. 设计导学案

根据微视频编写的阅读材料设计的导学案如下所示。

（1）Read these new words or phrases following the video.（观看视频后读这些新单词或短语。）

  treasure n.宝藏，珍宝   vineyard n.葡萄园

  eager v.渴望   illness n.疾病

  search for 寻找   bury-buried v.埋藏

  dig v.挖掘   juicy adj.多汁的

  plump adj.丰满的   sweet adj.甜美的

  reward n.报酬，报答

（2）Read the fable and mark the sentence T or F.（读寓言故事，判断正误并改正错误。）

① The grape grower has too hard working sons.（ ）

② The two sons were interested in learning growing grapes.（ ）

③ It was easy to find the treasure in the vineyard.（ ）

④ They continued to dig day and night although they didn't find the treasure.（ ）

⑤ The two sons found treasure at last.（ ）

（3）Watch the video, read the fable and then draw a mind map.（观看视频，阅读寓言故事并画出故事情节的思维导图，用单词或短语描述所画的图片。）

（4）After reading this fable, can you ask two more questions about it?（看完这个寓言后，你能再问两个问题吗？）

提的问题要有一定的意义。

Q1: _____

Q2: _____

（5）Can you predict what the two sons will be like in the future.（你能预测两个儿子的未来发展吗？）

_____

4. 师生开展活动

在课堂教学中，老师和学生一起进行了以下主要学习活动。

（1）学习理解类活动。

第一步，围绕主题，创设情境，铺垫语言。教师进行翻转检测，提出问题，在语境中激活相关的词汇。

第二步，概括、梳理、整合信息。学生细读课文，找到主人公的相关信息，梳理并整合细节信息，使之结构化，通过对细节信息的梳理，熟悉并学习一些固定搭配和本课特有的语言表达方式，最后给图片排序。

（2）应用实践类活动。

第三步，实践与内化所获得的语言知识和文化知识。学生依据所梳理和提炼的结构化知识，运用所学习的固定搭配或语言表达方式，阅读句子，并将它们按正确的顺序排列。

第四步，基于主题与内容进行分析与预测，表达个人观点。

①学生根据两个儿子的表现，感受他们父亲的情感变化。

②学生通过小组讨论预测两个儿子的未来。

③学生通过角色扮演，深度解读主人公的行为和情感态度。

（3）迁移创新类活动。

第五步，分析评价语篇的意义与形式。学生分小组分享各自的问题，然后尝试回答这些问题。

第六步，在新的语境中开展想象与创造，运用所学语言分析问题，解决问题。学生进行读后感分享。

本课例是一节翻转课堂的英语课外阅读课。课例中课前播放微视频，学生完成自主学习任务单；课堂中通过情景创设、小组合作等方式内化和运用所学内容，促使学生由被动学习变为主动学习，促使教学从侧重低阶思维培养转向侧重高阶思维培养。通过学习，学生对"真正的宝藏是努力付出"有了深层次的思考，形成了新的认知和思维品质。

（三）运用微视频，进行专题阅读教学

结合近期重要事件，进行相关的专题阅读教学，如经典演讲、名人传记等，运用相关微视频，有意识地帮助学生感悟其精神内涵，收获榜样力量，反思自己的人生成长，塑造自己的精神品质。

本课例将以我校某老师的一节公开课为例。结合物理学家霍金去世这一重要事件，教师开展了一节以Making a Difference为题的课外阅读教学课。在这节课中，巧妙地插播了关于霍金的三个微视频，环环相扣，步步追随，"润物细无声"地实现了该节课的教学目标：

1. 英语语言能力和学习能力

（1）学生能阅读长文章，并理解大意。

（2）学生能利用思维导图理清复杂的概念关系。

2. 文化品格

学生能了解霍金的人生经历及其人格魅力。

3. 思维品质

（1）学生能通过分析总结和推理出霍金的个人品质。

（2）学生能将这些优秀的品质迁移到自己的生活中。

在整个教学过程中，教师首先通过寒暄引出话题，接着在Pre-reading中，通过头脑风暴，激活学生对霍金的已有知识；在While-reading中，学生通过通

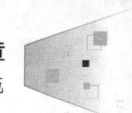

读全文,掌握文章大意,然后逐段阅读分析作者的写作意图和总结出主人翁的品质,再利用思维导图,理清段落中复杂的概念关系;其次在Post-reading中,学生总结出霍金的优秀品质,将这些品质迁移到自己的实际生活中,进行口头表述;最后是感情升华,老师通过播放霍金的原话微视频,在缅怀科学家的同时激励学生。

本案例合理科学地运用微视频层层推进教学,教学环节中呈现出的学科素养体现了教师对语篇的深入研读,很多内容都在原有的语篇基础上进行重新挖掘和梳理,重点突出,策略多样,精准高效,让英语课外阅读教学更有趣丰富,精准化教学贯穿课堂,让学生在快乐的小组合作探究中,逐步实现思维品质的形成和学习习惯的养成。

四、结语

这几个英语课外阅读教学课例展示的是基于英语学习活动观的教学设计。遵循这一活动观,教师需要整合课程的六要素,首先以主题为引领,以语篇为依托,将语言知识学习、文化内涵理解、语言技能发展和学习策略运用融合在学习理解、应用实践和迁移创新这三类相互关联的语言与思维活动中。学生在教师的引导下,概括出结构化知识,为进一步讨论主题意义奠定了语言文化和认知基础;其次学生尝试使用和内化所学的语言和信息,进行分析和欣赏,加深对主题意义的理解;最后是迁移和创新类活动,学生结合生活中可能面对的情景,通过多元和批判性思维,理性地表达自己的观点和态度。

我们不断求索的创造教育和智慧课堂,是现代信息技术手段与学科教学的深度融合,它能提升课堂学习效率,是"理解整体任务,聚焦核心问题"的实践活动;合理巧妙地运用微视频,使英语课外阅读教学课堂出现精准化学习发生,在学习过程中持续关注学生思维品质的形成和学习习惯的养成,更是基于培养学生的学习品质,不断创新智慧的课堂生态,以实现学生全面而个性化培养的教育追求。

玩转英语课堂的微视频
——初中英语课堂微视频的设计与实施

一、东莞市初中英语微课设计脚本

1. 基本信息

基本信息

微课名称	阅读微技能之根据配图预测文章大意	微课类型	阅读微技能
授课/制作人	郑艳霞	制作方式	录屏软件+PPT
适用对象	学生	时长	8分钟
教学目标	阅读微技能之根据配图预测文章大意,有两种方法: 1. 根据故事发生的时间、地点、人物、事件,预测文章大意。 2. 根据人物的身份、表情、神态、动作,预测文章大意。		
创新与亮点	1. 简单明了地把阅读的方法呈现出来。 2. 在讲解中练,在练习中归纳。 3. 所有的练习都有时代性、针对性。 4. 任何年级都适用。		

2. 设计与录制脚本

设计与录制脚本

微课基本信息	知识点名称	主旨大意题
	学科类型与教学对象	阅读策略、初三学生
	预计上课时间长度	10分钟

教学目标:指导学生掌握主旨大意题的解题技巧
教学资源与环境:PPT&QQ影音
教学过程:本微课把视频的流程设计为"三个步骤""三个特点""三种技巧"。 "三个步骤":①skimming跳读。②找主题句。③确定答案。 "三个特点":"精、准、全"。①精——语言精练,短小精悍。②准——能准确地表达作者的观点。③全——涵盖性强,能覆盖全文。 "三种技巧":一找、二比、三定。即①找主题句或高频词。②论字排辈,比比"谁大谁小"。③通过口诀、技巧点拨,使学生快速掌握主题的解题技巧,学生都兴趣盎然地沉浸在课堂教学中。

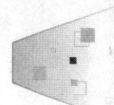

续表

| 设计理念与特色（微反思）：
首先，本堂课运用了微视频作为辅助手段，基于学生的认知规律，注意学生的阅读策略——跳读的培养，使学生在体验中学习和掌握主旨题的特点与解题技巧，体现新课改精神。
其次，通过口诀、技巧点拨，使学生快速掌握主旨题的解题技巧，大部分学生都能沉浸在课堂教学中。 |
|---|
| 微课制作方式：CS软件+PPT录屏。 |
| 专家点评：本节微课突出了主旨题的重点、突破了难点，生动有趣，对中考备考很有帮助。 |

二、"阅读理解之主旨大意题的解题技巧"微课教学设计方案

"阅读理解之主旨大意题的解题技巧"微课教学设计方案

教学步骤/活动	教学语言表述内容	多媒体配合方式与设计意图
如：Greeting & Learning goals	Predicting the gist by watching pictures（根据配图预测文章大意）
Tip1：根据故事发生的时间、地点、人物、事件，预测文章大意。
Tip 2：根据人物的身份、表情、神态、动作，预测文章大意。	多媒体配合方式：
PPT第1~3页。
设计意图：
清楚明了地介绍阅读方法，让学生一目了然。
Give examples	在练习中讲解两种方法如何操作。	多媒体配合方式：
①PPT第4~5页；②PPT第8~10页。
设计意图：
教师做示范，让学生有路可寻。
Practice	在练习中操练巩固。	多媒体配合方式：
①PPT第6~7页；②PPT第11~12页。
设计意图：
即学即练，即时巩固。
Summary	再次小结两种方法。	多媒体配合方式：
PPT第13~14页。
设计意图：
加深印象，让学生掌握方法。

三、优课课例1：Go For It 八年级下册 Unit 1 What's the matter？（Section A 3a）

（一）Analysis of Students（学情分析）

Students are familiar to this length of reading material, so it's not difficult for them to read the passage. And the new words and phrases are easy to understand. What's more, students are interested in stories, especially stories about daily life.

（二）Analysis of the Teaching Material（教材分析）

This is the second period of Unit 1. In the first period, students have learnt to talk about health problems and accidents, and they have also learnt to give advice. In this period, students need to learn about the reading material and give advice according to the situation.

（三）Teaching Goals（教学目标）

1. Target language

What's the matter?

I have a headache.

What's the matter with Ben?

He hurt himself.

Does he have a toothache?

Yes, he does.

What should she do?

She should take her temperature.

2. Ability goals

（1）To develop students' ability reading skills.

（2）To foster students' abilities of communication and their innovation.

（3）Learn to give advice in different situation .

3. Strategy goals

Task-based approach（任务型教学法）, Situational approach（情境教学法）, The communicative language teaching（交际教学法）.

4. Emotional goals

Learn to know how to help others when they are in trouble .

5. Teaching aid

A computer for multimedia use.（如下表）

（Teaching aid： A computer for multimedia use）

Teaching procedures

Steps	Teacher's activities	Students' activities	Ways
Step 1：Lead-in	Play a video about the situation that people are on the way to work or school.	Watch the video and take notes.	观看视频，引起学生注意，引入话题。
Step 2：Micro-course	Play a micro-course about reading skill.	Watch the micro-course and take notes.	观看微视频，学习阅读微技能：看图预测。
Step 3：Pre-reading	Guide the students to look at the picture in Page 3 and ask some questions. Read the title of the passage.	Talk about the picture and the title, predict the story.	看图预测，读题预测。
Step 4：While-reading	Show the students three questions.	Read the passage and answer the questions.	跳读文章，回答问题。
	Show the students exercise.	Read the passage again and choose the right answers.	细读文章，选择正确答案。
	Show the students exercise.	Check the things that happened in the story.	回顾全文，整体理解。
Step 5：Post-reading	Show the students questions.	Discuss the questions with a partner and try to give advice.	谈论故事情节，并给出建议。
	Show the students a mind-map.	Retell the story according to the mind-map.	看图复述故事。
Step 6：Summary	Sum up what we have learnt in today's lesson.	Try to use the reading skill.	复习巩固，学会阅读技巧。
Step 7：Homework	Write a continuation of the story.		

（四）课堂实录

Step 1：Lead-in

T：Everybody, how do you go to school every day? What about your parents, how do they go to work every day? Let's watch a video and then tell me how many transportations there are in the video.

（设计意图：通过观看视频，引起学生注意，引入本节课的话题。）

Step 2：Micro-course

T：Now let's watch a micro-course and answer the question：what's the reading skill?

（设计意图：通过学习微课，了解阅读微技能：看图预测。）

Step 3：Pre-reading

T：Look at the picture, what can you see in the picture? What are they doing?

（设计意图：通过看图，预测故事情节。）

T：Read the title of the passage, can you predict the story according to the picture and the title?

（设计意图：通过题目，预测故事情节。）

Step 4：While-reading

T：Read the passage as quickly as you can ,find out the answers to these questions.

　　Check the answers.

（设计意图：通过快速阅读文章，回答问题，了解文章大意。）

T：Read the passage again, find out the detail and choose the right answers. Check the answers.

（设计意图：通过细节阅读，理解文章。）

T：Now, read the following sentences, check the things that happened in the story. Check the answers.

（设计意图：通过判断句子，再一次整体理解文章。）

Step 5：Post-reading

T：What do you think of the driver? If you are there at that time, what will you do? Do you agree with the passengers? Talk with your partner.

（设计意图：通过问题讨论，学生表达自己的观点或给出建议，并达成一定的共识。）

T：Retell the story according to the mind-map.

（设计意图：通过复述故事，训练学生的表达能力，并进一步理解文章。）

Step 6：Summary

T：Now let's review what we have learned today. What reading skill do you know?

（设计意图：教师和学生的最后总结，让学生对自己今天学习的知识进行了梳理，又一次强化，加深印象。）

Step 7：Homework

Write a continuation of the story.（30 words）

（设计意图：通过续写故事，让学生表达自己的想法，并达到创新。）

（五）Teaching Reflection（教学反思）

本节课的故事从图片开始就引起了学生的兴趣。因此，以此为契机，引导学生通过看图预测故事情节，水到渠成，还有阅读中的任务设计也是体现跳读和细读这两个阅读微技能。由于文字的故事情节鲜明，因此在思维导图的帮助下，让学生复述故事也是比较容易的。其不足之处是由故事引申出来的问题：当别人遇到困难时"帮不帮"或者说"怎么帮"，这在课堂上没有进行较深入的讨论，老师也只是一笔带过。

四、优课课例2：2015年中考备课复习课——阅读理解

（一）Analysis of Students（学情分析）

Students are getting ready for the Junior high school graduation level examination. They have done all kinds of tests, but most students fail in the No.65. They don't know how to judge the main idea of a passage.

（二）Analysis of the Teaching Material（教材分析）

As for material for revision, we use the materials from the exams of the past years because they are formal and official.

（三）Teaching Goals（教学目标）

1. Target language

Reading material.

2. Ability goals

（1）To develop students' a bility of reading skills.

（2）To foster students' a bilities of communication and their innovation.

（3）Learn how to use the micro-skill to choose the right answer.

3. Strategy goals

Task-based approach（任务型教学法），Situational approach（情境教学法），The communicative language teaching（交际教学法）.

4. Emotional goals

Learn to know more about the reading skills.

5. Teaching aid

A computer for multimedia use.（如下表）

（Teaching aid：A computer for multimedia use）

Teaching procedures

Steps	Teacher's activities	Students' activities	Ways
Step 1：Organization and Warming up	Show students a table.	Read through the table.	明确考试结构，引入主题。
Step 2：Presentation	Show students a reading passage of 2012.	Read through the passage and find out the main idea of each paragraph.	举例分析。
Step 3：Micro-course	Show students a micro-course about reading skills.	Watch the micro-course and take notes.	观看微课，学习阅读微技能：主旨大意题。
Step 4：Practice	Show students a reading passage of 2014.	Read through the passage and find out the answer of No. 65.	运用阅读微技能完成题目。
Step 5：Conclusion	Sum up the feature of and the skills of this kind of question.	Review the feature and the skills.	复习巩固题型特点和答题技巧。

续表

Steps	Teacher's activities	Students' activities	Ways
Step 6: Exercise	Show students a reading passage of 2013.	Read through the passage and find out the answer of No. 65.	学以致用。
Step 7: Homework	Finish the six reading passages in student's sheet.		

（四）课堂实录

Step 1: Organization and Warming up

T: Look at the table. Can you find out the answers of these blanks? What is the topic in number 4? How many scores does it conclude? And what percentage is it?

（设计意图：通过了解中考试卷结构，清楚阅读理解所占比重，意识到阅读理解的重要性。）

Step 2: Presentation

T: Do you know Barbie? Here is a passage about Barbie. And the 65 question is "What is the best title of the passage?" Let read through the passage and find out the title. First, the first paragraph, what is it about? …and the second paragraph?

（设计意图：通过2012年广东中考第65题的主旨大意题引出本节课的重点。）

Step 3: Micro-course

T: Now let's watch a micro-course and learn the reading skill. How can we deal with this kind of problem?

（设计意图：通过观看微课，学习阅读微技能：主旨大意题。）

Step 4: Practice

T: From the micro-course, we know the ways of dealing with the question. Now try to finish this one.

（设计意图：通过2014年广东中考第65题，训练学生运用阅读微技能完成题目。）

Step 5: Conclusion

T: Now let's review what we have learned today. What is the feature of this kind of question? How can we deal with it?

（设计意图：教师和学生的最后总结让学生对自己今天学习的知识进行了梳理，又一次强化，加深印象。）

Step 6: Exercise

T: Now let's try again. Find out the answer of this question.

（设计意图：通过2013年广东中考第65题，训练学生运用阅读微技能完成题目。）

Step 7: Homework

Finish the six reading passages in student's sheet.

（设计意图：通过阅读训练，让学生巩固所学。）

（五）Teaching Reflection（教学反思）

本节中考复习课选题精准，特意选取学生在平时考试或作业中容易丢分的主旨大意题作为主题突破，所选材料均为历年广东中考题，训练目的性非常强。微课的阅读微技能的指导也非常精准，言简意赅。整节课讲练结合，精讲多练，学生的反馈也非常好，认为在学习了这种阅读技能之后，答题信心非常强。

第四章

专题语法的微视频设计与实施

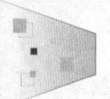
玩转英语课堂的微视频
——初中英语课堂微视频的设计与实施

语法微视频教学的技巧

《义务教育课程标准》在认知策略五级目标中有这样的描述："善于发现语言的规律，并能运用规律举一反三。"认知策略是指学生为了完成具体学习任务而采取的步骤和方法，其主要作用是优化人的认知过程，即认识事物和理解事物的过程。"语言之所以能够成为一种方便的交际工具，是因为它的系统性。语言的系统性反应在它有极强的规则性"。（束定方，1998）善于发现语言的规律并能运用规律举一反三，作为认知策略的具体描述形式，在把握学习方向、提高学习效率、形成自主学习的能力方面，具有重要的实践意义，是自主学习能力发展的主要渠道。

长期以来，英语语法的掌握是英语能力的基本功，而学生的英语语法的学习效果并不令人乐观。改进教学方法，培养学生善于发现语言规律和运用语言规律举一反三的能力，注重认知策略的有效性影响，是改善和提高英语语法教学效果的重要途径。随着经济社会的不断发展和科学技术水平的提高，微视频作为一种新的信息载体，在英语课堂的语法教学中起到了重要的作用，它使传统语法教学摆脱了机械死板的"填鸭式"教学方式，使语法教学情景化、具体化、"碎片化"，在一定程度上减轻了学习者的心理压力，另外从内化和外化两种角度，培养学生用观察、发现、归纳和实践等方法，发现语言规律，感悟语言功能，形成运用语言规律举一反三的能力，从而促进语言实践能力的提高。

那么，在英语课堂上，如何巧用、善用语法微视频，进行认知策略的渗透和培养，使学生善于发现语言规律，运用语言规律，提高语言实践能力呢？

在英语教学中渗透认知策略，培养学生善于发现语言规律，并能运用语言规律举一反三的能力，巧用善用语法微视频，可以从以下三个方面把握。

第四章
专题语法的微视频设计与实施

一、培养预习习惯

利用语法微视频，培养学生预习的习惯，借助联想把相关的知识联系起来。

"凡事预则立，不预则废"。做任何工作，事先都要做好充分的准备，英语学习也不例外，预习能为新知识的学习扫除障碍，提高学习质量，增强学生的自主意识。必要的预习，可以借助联想把相关知识联系起来，如对所学习的单词进行分类、借助语境学习词汇等，对所获得的信息进行有效的分类和储存，可以在遵循记忆规律的基础上提高记忆效果，也有利于发现语言规律。

下面以人教版《Go for It》七年级上册"Unit 6 Do you like bananas？"中的一段对话为例，说明利用语法微视频，培养学生预习的习惯，在语境中学习词汇，按照词语的形式分类，探究规律的方法。这段对话向学生展示"饮食"这一话题，重点难点是利用Do you like...? 句式和countable noun, uncountable noun进行情景交际。由于本课的词汇多数不是陌生词汇，大多在小学阶段学过，因此从发现语言学习规律出发，体验探究学习的角度思考，本环节的词汇学习，应该是让学生充分参与和感受，有效利用信息搭建从已知到未知的桥梁。所以在本课的词汇预习中，我预先播放了一个微视频，微视频的词汇导入活动是这样设计的：通过播放一首动画歌曲，引出今天学习的话题，同时活跃课堂气氛，然后创设一个情景，即介绍一个新朋友给学生，为下个环节做好铺垫。

案例：

T：After enjoying the music called *Look at those apples*, I'm sure you know today's topic—Food. Now I will introduce a new friend to you, its name is Foodman. So do you know which food he likes?

S：Milk, water, carrot, orange...

设计意图：兴趣是学好英语的关键。在课堂教学中，应抓住学生的心理，创设轻松的氛围，让学生消除紧张感，采用多种形式的归类方法，鼓励学生建立自己的词汇联想库。在学习一个单词时，同时教会学生学习同类词，把上面的内容按照词语的形式分类，学生就会有意识地去发现规律并总结规律。这种规律探究方法，有助于学生发现语言的规律，并能够运用规律举一反三，降低英语学习的难度，提高英语学习的效率，如下图所示。

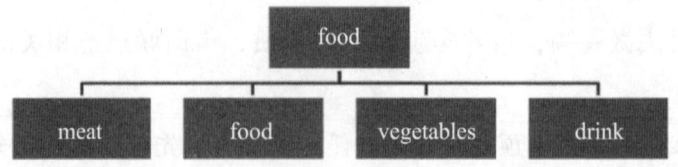

二、发现语言规律

善用语法微视频，培养学生通过观察、发现、归纳和实践等方法，发现语言规律，感悟语言功能。

语法是从语言实践中归纳出来的起组织作用的规则。懂得了语法就可以减少运用语言的盲目性，提高准确运用语言的能力，而语法教学能凸显语言的规律性，化繁为简，使学生少走弯路，有助于培养和提高学生的认知策略。适当地讲授语法知识，可以促使学生主动去理解、记忆和运用语言，自觉地进行练习，全面发挥认知学习的积极作用，提高学习的效果，有助于培养学生的自学能力和形成有效的学习策略。

例如，在学习《Go for It》八年级下册的后面三个单元时，由于语法项目都是关于现在完成时的，所以可以分别用三个语法微视频来进行介绍。第一个微视频可以是关于现在完成时的结构和用法的介绍以及练习；第二个微视频主要介绍现在完成时的标志词for和since的区别；第三个微视频则重点介绍延续性动词和短暂性动词的转换。每一个视频都针对一个特定的问题，有较强的针对性，这样既可以把现在完成时的知识点"碎片化"，化难为易，又可以在情境中介绍难点用法，进行系统的训练，这样就可以在三个具体情景中介绍完现在完成时，把难点分散、重点、突出，学生理解起来就容易多了。正如萨尔曼·汗所说："这种方式，它似乎并不像我站在讲台上为你讲课，它让人感到贴心，就像我们同坐在一张桌子面前，一起学习，并把内容写在一张纸上。"在课程讲授完毕之后，还提供习题、测试等供学习者加固知识点，例图如下图所示。

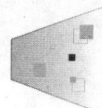

第四章
专题语法的微视频设计与实施

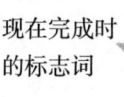

现在完成时的标志词

alreay, yet, never, just, ever, before, lately, twice, recently, so far, in the past few days..., since+..., for+...

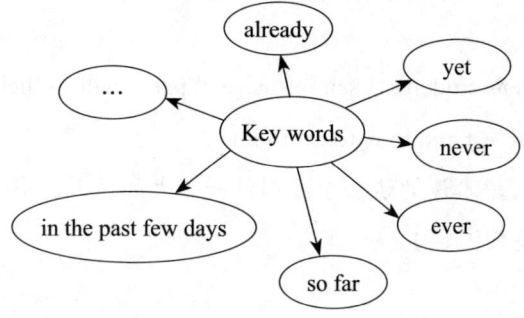

since & for 的用法区别：

- Since（自……以来）：
  ① since+时间点
    He has stayed here since 5 o'clock.
  ② since+从句
    She has taught English since he came here.
- For（长达）：
  for + 时间段
    He has kept the book for 2 weeks.

三、引导学生反思

巧用语法微视频，培养学生及时复习的习惯，引导学生进行阶段性的反思。

以被动语态的复习为例进行说明：被动语态是初中英语学习的一项重要的语法项目，同时也是学习的难点。本案例通过创设情境，引导学生发现语言形式和规律，并自觉运用规律进行语言实践。教师在核心环节1中，从一次毕业生晚会的饮食准备入手，巧妙地将饮食和习俗的学习融为一体，自然地引出了本课的语法项目——被动语态。通过必要的回忆和复习，使学生借助联想把相关知识联系起来，并对所获得的信息进行有目的的分类，有利于发现语言规律，运用规律，同时体现了被动语态在具体语境中的功能和意义。

77

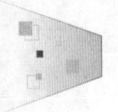

玩转英语课堂的微视频
——初中英语课堂微视频的设计与实施

案例：

毕业晚会上的"大餐"

一、核心环节1

Engage

The teacher tells students a school leavers' party will be held, asks students for advice about what to eat and how to eat them.

（设计意图：给本课的语法学习创设一个大的情景，引发学生对话题的关注，同时复习相关词汇。）

Presentation

T：What western table manners do you know?

S：Forks and knives are used when people eat western food...

（设计意图：回忆和复习上节课学过的内容，提示学生要用被动语态来表述。）

T：Translate some table manners of western food.

（1）人们吃西餐时使用刀和叉，左手拿叉右手拿刀，用叉子按住食物，再用刀切开，喝汤要用勺子。

（2）在开始进餐时，主人会让你自己夹菜。

（3）有些食物可以直接用手拿着吃。

（4）如果主人给你喜欢吃的东西，你可以把它放在盘子边上。

（设计意图：让学生在翻译的过程中体验中英文的差异，即主被动语态的使用差异，加深理解被动语态在语境中的功能和意义。）

二、核心环节2

T：Till now, can you tell me the different forms of passive voice ?

教师播放关于被动语态的微视频，在上述情景中，呈现被动语态的结构，完成设计的练习。

（设计意图：让学生自主总结归纳被动语态的各种形式，然后分别进行4组专项练习，使学生进一步巩固对被动语态结构的理解。）

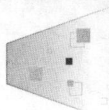

第四章
专题语法的微视频设计与实施

Activate

（1）Task 1

T: Well, compared with western table manners, can you say something about Chinese table manners?

Chopsticks, use, Chinese food

food, topic of conversation, good, can, consider

（设计意图：教师给出关键词，让学生通过连词成句的方式在语境下完成中国的就餐习惯的表达，既降低了学习难度，又激发了学生的思考意识，具有较强的可操作性。）

（2）Task 2

Ask the students to complete the passage:

Guests at a new restaurant in Dalian _____ (serve) by blind waiters, the guests can't see either, because the restaurant _____ (keep) dark. No lights _____ (allow), anything with a light must _____ (turn) off. The idea _____ (think) of five years ago. The idea says: "When the food can _____ (not see), so that the sense of taste _____ (improve)." "Don't worry that you won't enjoy food without seeing it. The enjoyment of the food _____ (make) possible by your nose, fingers, and ears instead." promises the restaurant owner. The restaurant _____ (run) for five years.

（设计意图：在理解语篇的基础上进一步理解并运用被动语态的不同形式。）

在英语课堂的语法教学上，相对于较宽泛的传统课堂，语法微视频的内容丰富、主题突出，更适合教师的需要："微视频"主要是为了突出课堂教学中某个知识点（如语法教学中重点、难点、疑点内容）的教学，内容更加精简。对学生而言，微视频能更好地满足学生对不同学科知识点的个性化学习，按需选择学习，既可查缺补漏又能强化巩固知识，是传统课堂学习的一种重要补充和拓展资源。特别是随着手持移动数码产品和无线网络的普及，基于微视频的移动学习、远程学习、在线学习、"泛在学习"将会越来越普及，其必将成为一种新型的教学模式和学习方式，它更是一个可以让学生自主学习，进行探究性学习的平台。

玩转英语课堂的微视频
——初中英语课堂微视频的设计与实施

在日常的语法教学中,教师要注意改变教学方式,引导学生体验语法结构在语境中的使用情况,让学生自己通过观察、归纳、总结去发现语法规则,再正确使用语法。同时,引导学生从表达需要出发,从观察语言形式入手,关注语言形式的表意功能和在实际语境中的作用。在归纳语法教学中,学生首先接触的是包含语法规则的真实情境,然后根据上下文的信息,归纳出使用规则。通过学习,归纳总结语言使用规律,可深化学生对用法的理解。因此,语法教学不是单纯的讲解和传授一些规则,更重要的是在语言实践中培养学生对结构和语言形式的敏感性,培养他们的语法意识,从而提高学生用语法知识自主发现、自主分析和自主学习的能力,促进他们学习过程中的内化,即通过发现语言规律,提高举一反三的能力,从而促进语言实践能力的提高。

初中语法微视频教学的具体实施

一、微视频教学的设计

以初中英语语法的现在完成时为例，根据现在完成时的知识点与难度，可以进行4个教学微视频的设计，即现在完成时构成、动词过去分词的变化、for 和 since 的区别和短暂性动词与延续性动词。"短暂性动词与延续性动词"微视频的教学设计（如下表所示）。

"短暂性动词与延续性动词"微视频的教学设计

微课基本信息	知识点名称	现在完成时的"短"与"延"
	教学对象	九年级学生
	预计上课时间长度	10分钟

教学目标：学会区别短暂性动词和延续性动词以及它们在现在完成时句子中的用法。
教学资源与环境：CS录屏软件。
教学过程： 1. 观察归纳：短暂性动词在肯定句、疑问句中不能与for、since引导的时间状语连用，常用相应的延续性动词来代替短暂性动词。 2. 巧记短暂性动词：开始离去借来还，出生入死买到家，穿衣入睡感冒，开开关关变结束。 3. 短暂性动词转换成延续性动词：4个变，其他用be表状态。 4. 实战实练。 5. 小结。
设计理念与特色： 运用逆向思维法，用口诀记住初中阶段常用的短暂性动词，然后用排除法进行句子运用。
呈现方式：CS软件录屏+声音。

玩转英语课堂的微视频
——初中英语课堂微视频的设计与实施

录制本节微视频,所用到的PPT设计如下图所示。

Micro Course

现在完成时的
"短"与"延"

找出现在完成时结构

1. Ann has opened her micro-blog.
2. Mike has had a new book for one year.
3. He has been here since 3 years ago.

● 短暂性动词在肯定句、疑问句中不能与 for, since 引导的时间状语连用。

● 常用相应的 *延续性动词* 来代替短暂性动词。

短暂性动词?

18 "罗汉"

第四章 专题语法的微视频设计与实施

18 "罗汉"齐齐聚

"开始离去借来还，出生入死买到家，穿衣入睡别感冒，开开关关变结束。"

1. begin / start		10. arrive	
2. leave		11. resch	
3. go		12. put on	
4. borrow / lend		13. fall asleep	
5. come		14. catch a cold	
6. return		15. open	
7. join		16. close	
8. die		17. become	
9. buy		18. end / finish	

短暂性动词的变形

1. begin / start	be on	10. arrive	be here
2. leave	be away from	11. resch	be here
3. go	be off	12. put on	wear
4. borrow / lend	keep	13. fall asleep	be asleep
5. come	be here	14. catch a cold	have a cold
6. return	be back	15. open	be open
7. join	be in	16. close	be closed
8. die	be dead	17. become	be
9. buy	have	18. end / finish	be over

学法指导：巧记短暂性动词及其转换

> 18 "罗汉"齐齐聚
> "开始离去借来还，出生入死买到家，
> 穿衣入睡别感冒，开开关关变结束。"

4个变，其他
用be表状态

Have a try

- 1. I am sorry, Jim. I __D__ your book for such a long time.
-   A. have borrowed   B. have lent
-   C. have returned   D. have kept
- 2. He __C__ London since five years ago.
-   A. have been away from   B. have left
-   C. has been away from   D. has left
- 3. How long have you __A__ here? About 2 months.
-   A. been   B. gone   C. come   D. arrived

★how long 提问的句子须用延续性动词

Summary

二、微视频在初中英语语法课中的应用

教学微视频应如何应用于实际教学中呢？基于其在教学中的辅助作用，可以把微视频分为Pre-Micro-video，While-Micro-video 和 Post-Micro-video这三方面来讲述其在语法课中的应用。

1. Pre–Micro–video（课前微视频）

在初中英语语法中，有一些语法知识比较难，知识点比较多，比如现在完成时态、被动语态和宾语从句等，仅靠一节语法课学生很难掌握好这些知识点。如果在学生接触这些知识点之前，教师提前布置学习任务，让学生自行观看相关知识点的微视频，通过微视频的观看可以达到预先学习的效果。当然，教

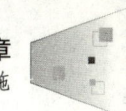

师布置观看任务的同时也应该布置检测观看结果的任务以评价学生的预习成果。有了这种微视频学习作为铺垫，课堂上再进行语法教学也就能得心应手了。

2. While–Micro–video（课中微视频）

相对于系统的语法学习，在日常的英语课堂教学中，我们会经常遇到一些语法知识点，如在听力课中遇到little 与few, 在阅读课中区别other、another、the other、others等。

3. Post–Micro–video（课后微视频）

课后微视频有利于进行语法复习，特别是中考语法复习，每名学生对不同知识点的掌握程度都不同，如果教师把同一个语法知识反反复复地讲解，对于已经掌握的学生来说就是浪费时间，炒冷饭。那么还不懂的学生怎么办呢？不讲解不行。课后学生可以根据自己的理解水平，选择所需的微视频进行"补救式"，以达到自己的学习目的。

一、初中语法微课教学设计举例（如下表所示）

《不定冠词a/an的区别》微课教学设计方案

微课基本信息	知识点名称	不定冠词a/an的区别
	教学对象	初中学生
	预计上课时间长度	5分钟
教学目标：区分不定冠词a/an的用法。		
教学资源与环境： 本节课用卡通片《天才眼镜狗》的预告片导入主题；以卡通片中的人物为基础，让学生由浅入深，步步深入区分a/an的用法。通过两个"技巧记忆"帮助学生更好地记住a/an的用法。		
教学过程：本节课是通过用"天才眼镜狗"为主线贯穿整节课，以它的人物形象导入新知识：①用"a"还是用"an"？②常见首字母不发音的单词。③5个元音字母前a/an 的选择。最后通过"我练我掌握"巩固a/an的用法。		
设计理念与特色： 1. 以电影《天才眼镜狗》的图片来进行情景导入，简单易懂。 2. 以两个"技巧记忆"帮助学生更好地记住不定冠词a/an的区别。 3. 巧用排除法，帮助学生更好地区分5个元音字母前用a/an的选择用法。		
微课制作方式：Camtasia studio。		

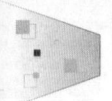

《现在完成时的"短"与"延"》微课教学设计方案

微课基本信息	知识点名称	现在完成时的"短"与"延"
	教学对象	九年级学生
	预计上课时间长度	10分钟

教学目标：学会区别短暂性动词和延续性动词以及它们在现在完成时句子中的用法。

教学资源与环境：PC终端，平板电脑，移动终端。

教学过程：
1. 观察归纳：短暂性动词在肯定句、疑问句中不能与for和since引导的时间状语连用，常用相应的延续性动词来代替短暂性动词。
2. 巧记短暂性动词：开始离去借来还，出生入死买到家，穿衣入睡别感冒，开开关关变结束。
3. 短暂性动词转换成延续性动词：4个变，其他用be表状态。
4. 实战实练。
5. 小结。

设计理念与特色：
运用逆向思维法，用口诀记住初中阶段常用的短暂性动词，然后用排除法进行句子运用。

微课制作方式：CS录屏软件+声音。

《现在完成时》微课教学设计方案

微课基本信息	知识点名称	现在完成时
	学科类型与教学对象	语法讲解、八年级学生
	预计上课时间长度	10分钟

教学目标：Enable students to master The Present Perfect Tense

教学过程：

Step One: Leading in Show the sad news of Malaysian Airline Flight MH370.

Step Two: Explain The Present Perfect Tense.

1. The form of The Present Perfect Tense.
2. The usages of The Present Perfect Tense.
3. The key words of The Present Perfect Tense.

Step Three: Summary.

Sum up what we have learned today.

Step Four: Exercises.

Do some exercises of The Present Perfect Tense.

Step Five: Promotion Look before you leap.

第四章
专题语法的微视频设计与实施

续 表

设计理念与特色:
1. 用积木块的形式讲解语法，把积木教学运用得淋漓尽致。
2. 现在完成时的用法是过去所发生的事情对现在造成的影响，对学生进行德育教育：三思而后行。

微课制作方式：CS录屏软件+声音

《情景交际——问路与指路》微课教学设计方案

微课基本信息	知识点名称	情景交际——问路与指路
	学科类型与教学对象	语法讲授、初三学生
	预计上课时间长度	8分钟

教学目标：复习情景交际用语——问路与指路

教学资源与环境：
本节微课利用学生们喜欢的《Dora-the explorer》这部动画片为素材制作，以轻松诙谐的方式讲解初中阶段学生须掌握的情景用语——问路与指路的用法。通过Dora和Boots去拯救王子的故事，带出本课学习内容，通过Dora闯过七关，帮助学生更好地记住问路、指路的常用句型。

教学过程：
片头（30秒以内）内容：以动画片的片头为开始，Dora和Boots出场创设微课情景——拯救王子之问路；通过Dora闯七关，让学生掌握情景交际用语——问路与指路的用法。

设计理念与特色（微反思）：本节微课利用学生们喜欢《Dora-the explorer》这部动画片为素材制作，以轻松诙谐的方式讲解初中阶段学生须掌握的情景用语——问路与指路的用法。以Dora和Boots救出王子的故事为终点，复习7种常用的问路与指路的句型。

微课制作方式：Microsoft PowerPoint 2010，Camtasia Studio，QQ影音。

专家点评：
本节微课利用学生们喜欢的动画片为素材制作，以轻松诙谐的方式讲解初中阶段学生须掌握的问路与指路的用法。以Dora和Boots拯救王子为故事起点，带出本课学习内容。本微课打破了传统授课沉闷无聊、生硬枯燥的模式，以一种轻松快乐的方式呈现出来，形式新颖，学生能够参与其中。但是只用一节微课来复习问路与指路的内容，很难做到面面俱到，想在最短的时间里让学生所学内容进行回顾和加强，只是一个尝试，还有很多地方需要思考和改进。

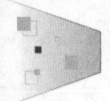

玩转英语课堂的微视频
——初中英语课堂微视频的设计与实施

《思维导图——语法复习的好帮手》微课教学设计方案

微课基本信息	知识点名称	思维导图——语法复习的好帮手
	教学对象	九年级学生
	预计上课时间长度	7分钟

教学目标:
认识思维和学习工具思维导图,并学习在语法复习中绘制和借助思维导图,提高复习效率。

教学资源与环境:PC终端,平板电脑,移动终端

教学过程:
1. 观察认识:思维导图的定义,结构和特点。
2. 学习绘制:以动词"说"和现在完成时为例,展示了如何在语法复习中,通过绘制思维导图,培养学生抓住关键词,理解知识内在结构,把一长串枯燥的语法表述文字变成有组织性的、可视的、容易记忆和理解的导图。
3. 实战演练:让学生自己动手绘制思维导图,以帮助学生提高语法的复习效率。
4. 小结。

设计理念与特色:
作为一种学习策略,把思维导图这种新型的记忆和思维方法运用到语法复习当中,培养学生抓住关键词、把握知识整体结构的能力,帮助学生理解知识的内在联系,提高语法的复习效率。

微课制作方式:CS录屏软件+声音

《定语从句难点突破》微课教学设计方案

微课基本信息	知识点名称	定语从句难点突破
	学科类型与教学对象	语法讲授、九年级学生
	预计上课时间长度	10分钟

教学目标:
1. 区分that 与which。
2. 关系代词省略问题。
3. 介词前置。
4. 一致问题。

教学资源与环境:平板电脑,电脑Windows XP系统,PPT。

教学过程:
1. 定语从句的基本概念。
2. 关系词只用that,不用which的情况。
3. 关系代词省略的情况。

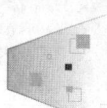

续 表

4. 介词后面的关系词。 5. 定语从句谓语与先行词在数上保持一致。 6. 小练兵。 7. 小结。	
设计理念与特色（微反思）： 本节微课主要根据东莞市中考英语对定语从句的考查要求，区分关系代词，并在此基础上，结合常见的几种情况进行分析，理论结合实例，语言简练，讲练结合。	
微课制作方式：CS软件+PPT录屏。	
专家点评：本节微课能够理论联系实际，结合实例与练习，明确区分关系词的用法，语言简练，通俗易懂。	

《被动语态难点突破——含有省略to的动词不定式做宾补的被动语态》
微课教学设计方案

微课基本信息	知识点名称	含有省略to的动词不定式做宾补的被动语态
	学科类型与教学对象	语法讲授、九年级学生
	预计上课时间长度	10分钟

教学目标：掌握怎样将含有省略to的动词不定式做宾补变为被动语态。	
教学资源与环境：PPT、电脑Windows XP以上系统、暴风影音。	
教学过程： 1. 引入。介绍Coco 和Doudou。 2. 知识点讲解。怎样将含有省略to的动词不定式做宾补变为被动语态。 3. 实战演练。 4. 中考链接。 5. 总结。	
设计理念与特色（微反思）： 本节课采用的是小孩与她的机器人玩具作为本节课的切入点，通过对出现的句子进行讲解和加入口诀进行记忆，再通过实战演练和中考链接进行知识巩固，最后达到学习本微课的教学目标。	
微课制作方式：CS软件+PPT录屏。	
专家点评： 本微课作品通过小孩和机器人玩具之间的关系和对话进行语法知识的引入和讲解，本节课重点突出了重难点，简化了难点，通俗易懂，与中考紧紧联系在一起，达到了教学目标。	

玩转英语课堂的微视频
——初中英语课堂微视频的设计与实施

《初中英语八年级下册 Unit 9 Section A 语法结构及运用》
微课教学设计方案

微课基本信息	知识点名称	初中英语八年级下册 Unit 9 Section A 语法结构及运用
	学科类型与教学对象	语法讲授、八年级学生
	预计上课时间长度	8分钟

教学目标：掌握现在完成时的构成、一般疑问句形式、肯定和否定回答，ever 和 never 的运用。

教学资源与环境：PPT、电脑Windows XP以上系统、暴风影音。

教学过程：
1. 引入。以寒假即将来临，Echo 想要去旅游作为引子。利用 Echo 和 Richard 的对话引出本节课的知识点——现在完成时。
2. 语法讲解。Never 和 ever 的区别。
3. 活学活用。
4. 音乐和美图欣赏。从音乐和美图引出第二个现在完成时的对话。
5. 语法讲解。
6. 玩转现在完成时。
7. 总结。

设计理念与特色（微反思）： 八年级下册Unit 9这个单元是以旅游为主线，以现在完成时的学习为语法功能。为了更好地体现这一个教学目标，本节课由寒假即将来临，Echo 想要外出旅游作为引子，引入了现在完成时的对话，并从现在完成时的句子中，总结出ever和never的用法，在此基础上配上练习进行巩固；然后从对话的内容引入到video-Echo 去哈尔滨旅游的照片，配上do you want to build a snowman 的音乐，进而引入另外关于现在完成的肯定回答——一个对话，通过对话的内容总结出现在完成时的构成，一般疑问句，和肯定、否定回答，接着进行相对应的练习，最后以对整个微课的总结作为结尾。

微课制作方式：CS软件+PPT录屏+会声会影视频制作。

专家点评： 本节微课采用了积木式教学，用不同颜色的积木突出了语法的不同成分，使语法讲解简单易懂。本微课虽然只有10分钟，但语法讲解透彻，而且还设计了音乐和图片欣赏，这改变了枯燥的语法学习，缓解了学生的压力，增强了学生的学习兴趣。

二、优课课例1：Go For It八年级下册Unit 9 Have you ever been to a museum? （听说课）

（一）Analysis of Students（学情分析）

Though students have learnt about travelling, they are still fond of it. And they have also learnt about talking about past experiences, so we don't need to worry about their words and phrases and expressions.

（二）Analysis of the Teaching Material（教材分析）

Students have learnt to talk about past events by using the simple past tense. In Unit 8, they have learnt the basic structure of the present perfect tense to talk about recent events and experiences. So it's easy for students to talk about past experiences. The difficult point is that the structure of the present perfect tense with been, ever and never.

（三）Teaching Goals（教学目标）

1. Target language

Have you ever been to a science museum?

No, I've never been to a science museum.

Have you ever visited the space museum?

Yes, I have. I went there last year.

I've never been to a water park.

Me neither.

2. Ability goals

（1）To develop students' ability of listening and speaking skills.

（2）To foster students' abilities of communication and their innovation.

（3）Learn to talk about past experiences by using the present perfect tense.

3. Strategy goals

Task-based approach（任务型教学法）, Situational approach（情境教学法）, The communicative language teaching（交际教学法）.

4. Emotional goals

Learn to know about travelling politely.（如下表所示）

（Teaching aid: A computer for multimedia use）

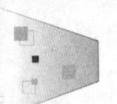

Teaching procedures

Steps	Teacher's activities	Students' activities	Ways
Step 1: Organization and Warming up	Play a music.	Listen and enjoy the music.	听歌曲热身，引入主题。
Step 2: Micro-course	Play a micro-course about the different structures of the present perfect tense.	Watch the micro-course and take notes.	观看微课，学习现在完成时的语法结构及运用。
Step 3: Picture talking	Show students a picture of this unit and ask questions about the picture.	Answer the questions according to the picture.	看图回答问题，引出目标句型。
Step 4: Listening	Play the tape for students to listen and check the boxes in 1b.	Listen and check the boxes in 1b.	听录音选择。
	Play the tape for students to listen and circle the places they hear in 2a.	Listen and circle the places they hear in 2a.	听录音画圈。
	Play the tape for students to listen and circle T for true or F for false in 2b.	Listen and circle T for true or F for false in 2b.	听录音判断。
Step 5: Pair-work	Show a conversation sample for students.	Make conversations about the places according to the sample in 2c in pairs.	两人对话，合作学习。
Step 6: Task work	Play the tape and show students two questions.	Listen to the tape and answer the questions.	通过对话练习听力。
	Give students task to role-play the conversation.	Role-play the conversation.	分角色扮演，合作学习。
Step 7: Summary	Sum up what we have learnt in today's lesson.	Review the different structures of the present perfect tense.	复习巩固，加深印象。
Step 8: Homework	Role-play the conversation in 2d and finish the exercise in the students' workbook.		

（四）课堂实录

Step 1： Organization and Warming up

T： Listen to a song, do you know the singer?

（设计意图：通过听Westlife的英文歌曲Seasons in the sun引入话题。）

Step 2： Micro-course

T： Let's watch a micro-course about the present perfect tense and finish the exercise in the student's sheet.

（设计意图：通过学习微课，了解现在完成时的语法结构以及用法。）

Step 3： Picture Talking

T： Look at the picture in P65. How many places can you see in the picture? Have you ever been to these places?

（设计意图：通过看图回答问题，引入本节课的目标句型。）

Step 4： Listening

T： Claudia and Sarah are talking about their past experiences. Have they ever been to these places? Check the boxes in 1b.

（设计意图：通过听录音，练习听力，熟悉目标句型的运用。）

T： Here is a map of the town in P66. Listen to the tape and circle the places you hear.

（设计意图：通过听录音，练习听力，熟悉目标句型的运用。）

T： Listen to the tape again and circle T for true or F for false in 2b.

（设计意图：通过听录音，进一步理解听力内容，熟悉目标句型的运用。）

Step 5： Pair-work

T： Have you ever been to the space museum?

S1： No, I haven't.

T： Have you ever been to the space museum?

S2： Yes, I have.

T： Now work with your partner, ask and answer the questions like this.

（设计意图：通过同桌对话，合作学习，运用目标句型。）

Step 6： Task

T： Listen to the tape and answer the following questions.

（设计意图：通过听录音，回答问题，练习听力。）

T：Read the conversation together and role-play it.

（设计意图：通过朗读对话，熟悉内容并进行角色扮演，让学生进一步理解句型的运用场景。）

Step 7：Summary

T：Now let's see what we have learnt in today's lesson. What structures of the present perfect tense do you know?

（设计意图：教师和学生的最后总结让学生对自己今天学习的知识进行了梳理，又一次进行了强化，加深了印象。）

Step 8：Homework

Role-play the conversation in 2d and finish the exercise in the students' workbook.

（设计意图：课后角色扮演，增加学生练习听说的机会，笔头练习是为了巩固现在完成时的语法结构及用法。）

（五）课后反思

本节听说课是一节常规的听说课，但由于加入了微视频的学习，所以课堂容量一下子大了起来，而且现在完成时的语法结构及运用通过微课的形式学习，使课堂不再单调乏味。不足之处在于，学生的训练都是在教师的掌控下进行，缺乏学生自己的东西。

三、优课课例2：Go For It 八年级下册Unit 10 I've had this bike for three years.（语法课）

（一）Analysis of Students（学情分析）

Students like to share their possessions with their friends. In this lesson, the language goal is talking about possessions and things around you. Students can use "I have...", "There is/are..." to express themselves.

（二）Analysis of the Teaching Material（教材分析）

In the last two units students have learnt the present perfect tense with already and yet, with been, ever and never, and they have known the basic structures. In this lesson, they are going to learn the present perfect tense with since and for.

（三）Teaching Goals（教学目标）

1. Target language

How long have you had that bike over there?

I've have it for three years.

How long has his son owned the train and railway set?

He's owned it since his fourth birthday.

Have you ever played football?

Yes, I did when I was little, but I haven't played for a while now.

2. Ability goals

（1）To develop students' ability of grammar.

（2）To foster students' abilities of communication and their innovation.

（3）Learn to use the present perfect tense in certain situation.

3. Strategy goals

Task-based approach（任务型教学法），Situational approach（情境教学法），The communicative language teaching（交际教学法）.

4. Emotional goals

Learn to know more about the collections of the museum and try to protect them.（如下表所示）

（Teaching aid：A computer for multimedia use）

Teaching procedures

Steps	Teacher's activities	Students' activities	Ways
Step 1：Organization and Warming up	Play a video about the Museum of terra-cotta warriors.	Watch the video and enjoy the collections.	观看视频，引入话题。
	Show an adv. about the narrators wanted to students.	Read the adv. and learn the background of the museum.	阅读招聘广告，了解背景。
Step 2：Micro-course	Play a micro-course about the present perfect tense.	Watch the micro-course and complete the student's sheet.	观看微课：现在完成时的"短"与"延"，完成练习。

续表

Steps	Teacher's activities	Students' activities	Ways
Step 3: Task	Introduce a 65-year-old teacher to the class. Guide the students to help the teacher to apply for the job of a narrator of the museum.	Learn about the teacher Work in group of four and try to organize the words according to the teacher's tips.	背景学习，小组合作，运用目标语言。
Step 4: Sharing	Ask students to share their words in the class and choose the best.	Share the words in the class.	分享成果，进行评价和自我评价。
Step 5: Self-learning	Ask students to write down the sentences about the present perfect tense.	Write down the sentences about the present perfect tense by themselves.	独立写句子，进行自我理解与消化。
Step 6: Exercise	Show students exercise about the present perfect tense.	Finish the exercise and check the answers.	练习、巩固与理解。
Step 7: Summary	Sum up what we have learnt in today's lesson.	Review the usage of the present perfect tense with since and for.	总结巩固语法规律。
Step 8: Homework	Ask students to finish the exercise about the present perfect tense.		

（四）课堂实录

Step 1: Organization and Warming up

T: Here is a video about the museum of terra-cotta warriors. Watch it and enjoy the collections in the museum.

（设计意图：通过观看西安兵马俑博物馆的视频，理解博物馆的藏品，引入情节。）

T: Here is an advertisement about the narrator wanted for the museum, read it and learn the requirements.

（设计意图：通过阅读博物馆招聘解说员的广告，铺设本节课的情节。）

Step 2: Micro-course

T: Let's watch a micro-course about the present perfect tense with since and for, and complete the exercise.

Check the answers.

（设计意图：通过学习微课，了解现在完成时的"短"与"延"的用法，为下一步任务打下语言基础。）

Step 3：Task

T： Mr. Li is a 65-year-old teacher of history. He has retired and he wants to look for a job as for his interests. And the collections in the museum are his favorite.

（设计意图：通过介绍退休教师李老师的情况引入任务。）

T： Can you help him？ Mr. Li wants to apply for the job as a narrator for the museum. Work in group of four, work out how Mr. Li should introduce himself and the collections in the museum.

（设计意图：通过小组合作学习，运用目标句型，帮助李老师想出最佳面试方案。）

Step 4：Sharing

T： Sharing time. Choose one student in your group to share your work and then select the best one.

（设计意图：通过分享学习成果，对照自己的学习，进行评价和自我评价。）

Step 5：Self-learning

T： Write down the sentences with the present perfect tense with since and for on your paper and check with your partner.

（设计意图：通过写句子进一步巩固现在完成时的句子结构。）

Step 6：Exercise

T：Finish the exercise in your sheet.

Check the answers.

（设计意图：通过完成相关时态的练习，巩固所学。）

Step 7：Summary

T：Now let's review what we have learned today. Do you know the present perfect tense with since and for?

（设计意图：教师和学生的最后总结让学生对自己今天学习的知识进行了梳理，又一次进行了强化，加深了印象。）

Step 8: Homework

Ask students to finish the exercise about the present perfect tense.

（设计意图：通过布置笔头作业，进一步巩固语法知识。）

（五）教学反思

本节课有两个亮点：一是在情景中学习语法，使沉闷、单调的语法学习有血有肉；二是微课运用得恰到好处，微课融入情景一点也不违和，而且微课对现在完成时的"短"与"延"讲解得清楚明了，本节课的难点通过微课来突破了，不足之处是学生的语法练习偏少，形式单调。

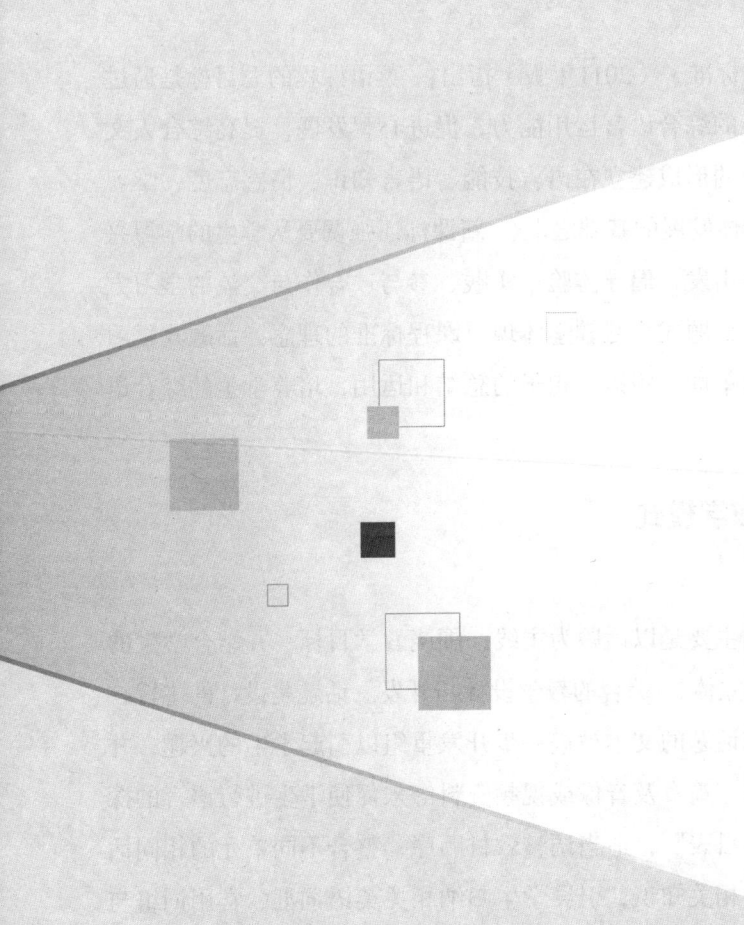

第五章 话题写作的微视频设计与实施

话题式微课教学的设计

《义务教育英语课程标准》（2011年版）指出，英语课程的总目标是通过英语学习使学生形成初步的综合语言运用能力，促进心智发展，提高综合人文素养，综合语言运用能力的形成建立在语言技能、语言知识、情感态度、学习策略和文化意识等方面整体发展的基础之上。新课标还强调要从学生的学习兴趣、生活经验和认知水平出发，倡导体验、实践、参与、合作与交流的学习方式和任务型的教学途径。话题式复习教学体现了课程标准的理念，话题式复习教学通过对话题所涉及的单词、短语、句子的总结和运用，培养学生的综合语言运用能力。

一、话题式复习教学模式

（一）特点

话题式复习教学模式主要是以话题为主线，围绕教学目标，并结合学生的具体情况和教材特点进行立体、综合的教学设计与开发。话题是设计的主旨，通过围绕主题线索和支撑话题的文本被进一步开发重组以引起学生的兴趣，并且利用与话题相关的文本、篇章及音像或视频资料等来促使学生进行语言的探索和学习。依据"话题项目表"，适当调整教材顺序，整合不同单元的相同话题，重组教学内容，综合相关知识，引导学生归纳相关英语词汇、常用词组与重点句型等，并围绕相关的话题进行活学活用，从而使更多的学生融入话题式复习教学模式的学习活动中，提高英语复习课的效率。

（二）作用

话题式复习教学，以话题为主要线索，将语法知识、语言技能等有机融合

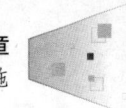

在一起，并以技能训练为主要目的，搭配一定的语法项目的点拨总结以及习题训练，这种教学打破了传统"讲授、操练与反馈"的教学模式，将《新课程标准》的教学理念融入其中，整合学生自主学习与合作学习模式，从而使复习课堂得以优化，提高复习教学质量与效率。

二、微课教学模式

（一）微课的概念

"微课"指按照《新课程标准》及教学实践的要求，以视频为主要载体，将教师在课堂内外教育教学过程中围绕某个知识点或教学环节而开展的精彩教与学活动的全过程记录下来。

"微课"的核心组成是课堂教学视频（课例片段），同时还包含与该教学主题相关的教学设计、素材课件、教学反思、练习测试及学生反馈、教师点评等辅助性教学资源。

（二）微课的主要特点

1. 微课"位微不卑"

微课虽然短小，比不上一般课程宏大丰富，但是它意义非凡、效果明显，是一个非常重要的教学资源。

2. 微课"课微不小"

微课虽然短小，但它的知识内涵和教学意义非常大，有时一个短小的微课比几十节课都有用。

3. 微课"步微不慢"

微课都是小步子原则，一个微课讲解一两个知识点，看似很慢，但稳步推进，实际效果并不慢。

4. 微课"效微不薄"

微课有积少成多、聚沙成塔的作用，通过不断的微知识、微学习，从而达到大道理、大智慧。

微课教学和话题式复习教学模式都有着不同的特点，接下来本文将以 Chinese Culture 这个话题作文课的设计将这两种教学模式巧妙地结合在一起，提高九年级的英语复习教学效率。

三、微课在话题式复习教学中的应用

在话题式复习教学中,为了使学生能够更好地通过该节课达到目的——产出,也就是最后的一个教学步骤,那么在前面的教学环节中就必须有足够的输入。基于话题式复习教学的这个特征,微课可以设计在话题作文复习课的开始。本文以Chinese Culture这个话题作文课的设计为例。

(一)微课的设计

随着中国的日益发展,中国的国际地位不断提高,我们的荣誉感也越来越强。我们要以身为中国人而感到自豪,要勇敢地向外国朋友介绍中国,使他们更加了解中国。设计时,首先考虑学生的知识水平,并且把初中已学的一些知识点进行整合,这样既可以帮助学生温故而知新,又可以使课堂简单易懂。

首先,对中国做一个基本介绍。结合《Go For It》教材八年级下第七单元的内容,设计如下内容(如下图所示)。

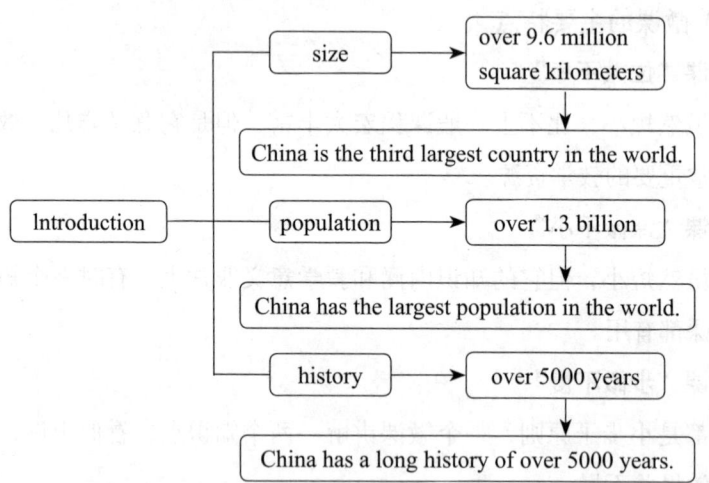

由此引出:

China is the third largest country in the world.

China has the largest population in the world.

China has a long history of over 5,000 years.

这为后面介绍中国的基本情况做好了铺垫。

其次,介绍中国的习俗。向外国朋友介绍中国,让他们了解中国的习俗。

有哪些习俗是外国朋友迫切需要了解的？结合《Go For It》教材九年级第十单元的内容（如下图所示）。

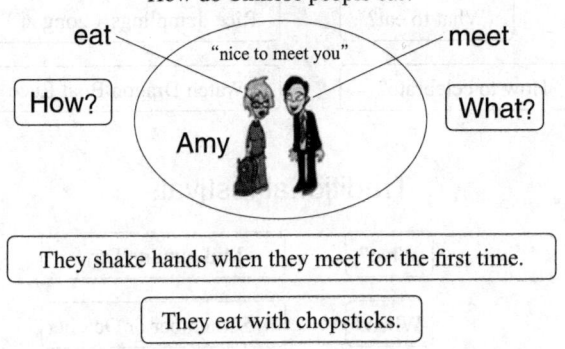

除了这些内容之外，我们还可以向外国朋友介绍中国的传统节日。在所有的中国的节日中，学生最了解的是三个节日：春节、端午节和中秋节，而且在《Go For It》教材九年级第二单元的内容中也向学生介绍了中秋节。那么，在微课中，设计三个节日的介绍，分别从what，when，what to eat，how to celebrate这四个要点来介绍，掌握了这四个要点，对于节日的介绍就易如反掌了（如下图所示）。

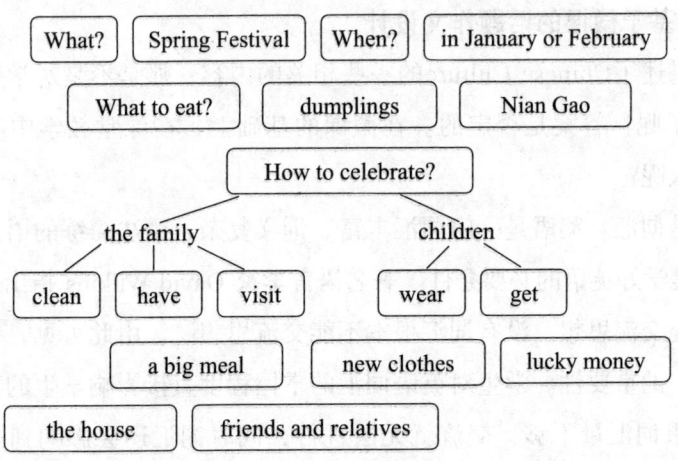

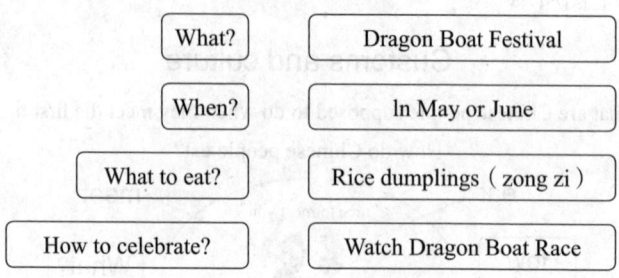

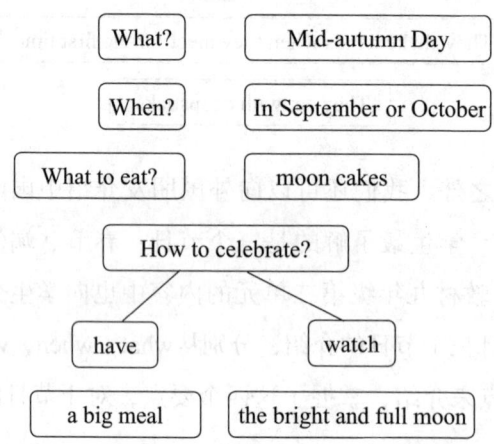

最后，本微课对前面所讲的内容进行了总结。这就是整个微课的设计。

（二）基于微课的话题作文设计

微课讲述了Chinese Culture的一些相关的内容，那是不是对学生已经有足够的输入了呢？答案是否定的。在微课的基础上，在课堂教学中应如何进行足够的输入呢？

首先是词汇。英语是一门词汇丰富、词义复杂、语法简练的语言，英语词汇的学习是学好英语的必要条件。著名语言学家David Wilkins指出，"没有语法几乎不能交流思想，没有词汇根本不能交流思想"。由此可见，词汇在英语学习过程中的重要性。学生对英语词汇的掌握程度直接影响学生的英语水平，学习者如果词汇量不够，交流就无法进行，同时词汇还会影响到一个人听、说、读、写各方面的能力，因此词汇在英语教学过程中起着十分重要的作用。

第五章
话题写作的微视频设计与实施

要想写好一篇话题作文，一定要有充足的词汇基础。设计怎样的词汇更适合呢？在微课中出现了很多与 Chinese Culture 有关的词汇，何不汇总这些词汇呢？这既可以复习微课里的词汇，又可以为后面的写作做好准备，一举两得。在这里把前面的词汇汇总在同一个幻灯片上作为一个课堂任务（如下图所示）。

Task Two Words

面积 ——— ☐	千米 ——— ☐
国家 ——— ☐	世界 ——— ☐
人口 ——— ☐	历史 ——— ☐
地点 ——— ☐	节日 ——— ☐
饺子 ——— ☐	朋友 ——— ☐
亲人 ——— ☐	习俗 ——— ☐
文化 ——— ☐	筷子 ——— ☐
拜访 ——— ☐	庆祝 ——— ☐
历史的 ——— ☐	传统的 ——— ☐

除了单词之外，学生可能对一些词组和句型没有掌握，特别是有关节日的正确表达。接着我设计了一个课堂任务，以便学生更好地掌握这些短语（如下图所示）。

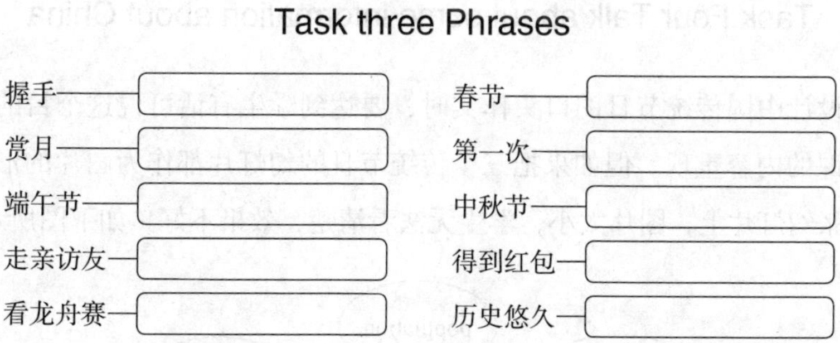

Task three Phrases

握手 ——— ☐	春节 ——— ☐
赏月 ——— ☐	第一次 ——— ☐
端午节 ——— ☐	中秋节 ——— ☐
走亲访友 ——— ☐	得到红包 ——— ☐
看龙舟赛 ——— ☐	历史悠久 ——— ☐

其次是口头作文。词汇这个地基已经打好了，现在需要支架，可以通过"说"也就是口头作文这个环节来搭建这个支架。通过"说"的环节既可以提高口语表达能力，为口语考试——中考的重要部分做好准备，又可以为后面的笔头作文做好铺垫。根据微课的内容，设计了学生"说"中国的基本情况和中国的传统节日（如下图所示）。

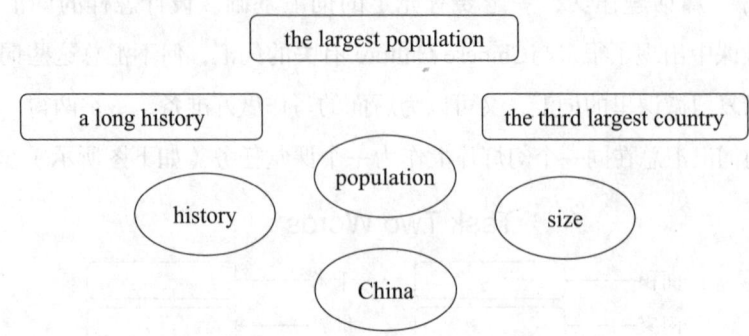

在设计这一个课堂任务时，需要对学生出现的错误有预见性。学生可能会对应该用has还是is产生疑惑，那么在口头作文之前，我先让学生明白has和is的运用（如下图所示）。

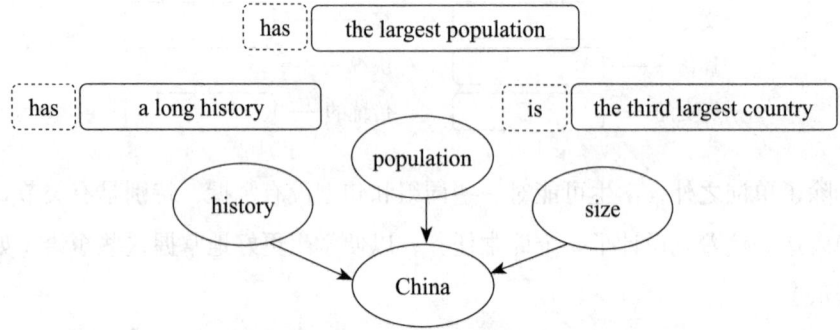

Task Four Talk about some information about China

在设计中国传统节日的口头作文时，要达到学生有话可说这个目的，必须要让微课的内容重现。但如果把三个传统节日的幻灯片都作为图片的形式出现在同一张幻灯片上，图片太小，学生无法看清楚，效果不好（如下图所示）。

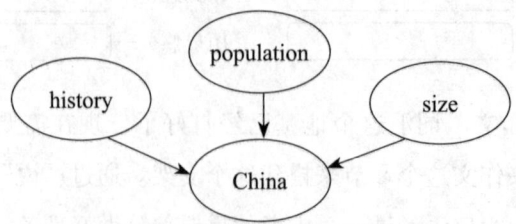

Task Four Talk about some information about China

When? | What to eat? | How to celebrate?

最后，应该怎样把这三张幻灯片作为图片出现在同一个幻灯片上呢？经过不断地调整和不同方法的尝试，我用会声会影把三张图片制作成影片出现在同一个幻灯片上，学生可以选择任一节日来跟同学一起谈论，这样保证了图片的清晰（如下图所示）。

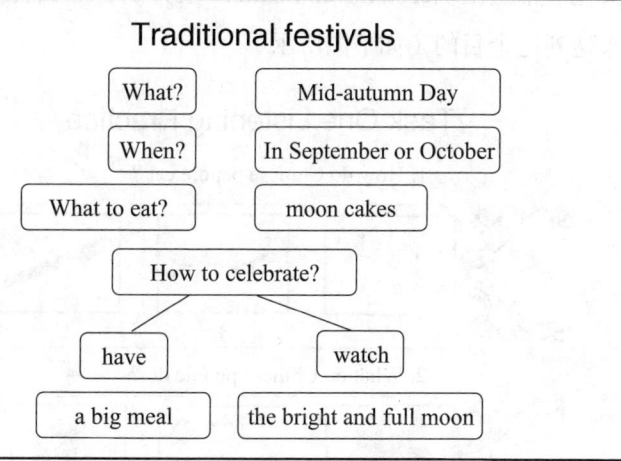

教学到这一环节，基本上已经将微课上所有的内容跟整个话题结合在一起了，为后面的话题作文做好了充足的准备。紧接着如何设计话题作文的题目呢？前面的环节和活动都是为最后一步做准备的。根据前面的铺垫设计为：Write a composition about China.

作为中国人，我们很自豪，请根据下面的提示写一篇介绍中国的文章，欢迎外国朋友到中国。

内容包括：①中国的基本情况介绍（至少两点）；②中国习俗的介绍（至少两点）；③你最喜欢的中国节日的介绍（what, when, what to eat, how to celebrate）。

到了这个环节，基本上已经将整个话题所要掌握的内容和环节完成了。本节课的设计是不是已经完美了呢？

（三）后期的修改

试上了本课件之后，我发现没有什么亮点，因此做了如下修改。

1. 融入听力

话题复习不仅可以为口语和读写综合服务，还可以提高听的能力。所有的听力都是围绕不同的话题来展开的，所以在本节课中可以融入听力。跟听力有关的中国文化经常是围绕customs and culture展开的，那么我就根据微课的内容设计听力来达到这个目的（如下图所示）。

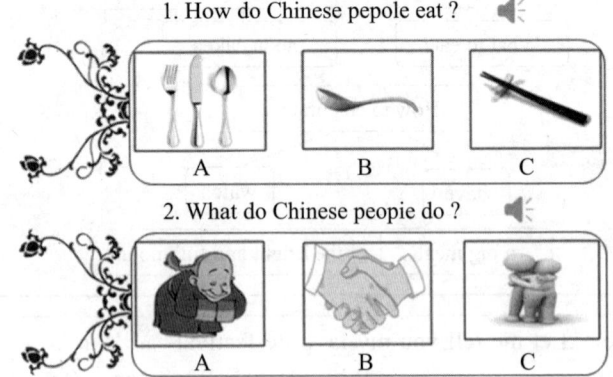

那么，听力这个环节究竟放在哪里更加合适呢？是否可以放在微课后面？如果放在后面，微课已经讲到了，那听是多余的。最后我决定将这个环节放在微之之前，听完材料后不立刻校对答案，让学生学习微课然后再找出答案。将听力作为引入，使微课与课件紧密结合在一起。

2. 插入歌曲

中国历史悠久，土地辽阔，人口众多，我们为自己是中国人而自豪。外国人怎样看待中国呢？插入一首由外国朋友唱的《China Dream》，这首歌讲述的是真实的故事以促进我们中学生更加爱国。将这首歌插入到口头作文和话题作文之间，可以让大脑稍微休息，也可以为后面的作文做铺垫。

3. 介绍写作技巧

（1）指导学生把握重点，找出各个点的关键词，明确写作任务。

（2）展示给分板，划分好分值，使学生留意每个点的重要性。

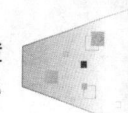

（3）强调如何写好开头与结尾。根据作文的提示教学生怎样写好开头和结尾。

4. 加强学生互改，促进合作学习

平时在作文课中，我们都采用老师批改的形式。但如果让学生互改，从同学中的作文当中找出错误，防止自己犯错，这种效果会更好。增加的这个学习任务在小组合作学习的形式下实现。

5. 总结和汇总学生的错误

学生在写作中，会出现一种情况，即所有的关键点都已经体现在作文上，但因为一些语法小错误而与满分作文失之交臂。那么，如何避免这种情况呢？在学生互改作文的同时，增加一个任务，将改的作文中的一两个错误写下来，老师再将其汇总，一起纠错。下面列举学生抄下来的一些句子。

China is a big country with long history.

People in China eat food with chopstick.

They always shake hand when they meet the first time.

汇总之后，本人将其展示，并让学生一起纠错。

改正后的句子为:

China is a big country with a long history.

People in China eat food with chopsticks.

They always shake hands when they meet for the first time.

（四）反思

通过这一整节课的设计，过程比较流畅，充分地将微课和课堂教学紧密地联系在一起。下面这两篇文章摘自学生的当堂作文。

Example One：

Hello, everybody, I am Li Ming. I'm Chinese. I'm proud of being a Chinese. Here I want to tell why I'm so proud.

China has the largest population in the world. It's a big country with long history.①

People in China eat food with chopsticks and they always shake hands when they meet for the first time.

Now, let me say something about my favorite festival. My favorite festival is the Spring Festival.② It's in January or February. People have a big meal that day. We wear new clothes and children can get lucky money from adults. What a great country China is! If you want to go aboard, China will be you best choice.

Example Two：

Hello, everybody, I am Li Ming. I'm Chinese. I'm proud of being a Chinese. Here I want to tell why I'm so proud.

China has a long history. China has the largest population in the world. China is the third biggest in the world.

In china, there are many manners. For example, we always shake hands when we meet for the first time. And we eat with chopsticks.

I love Dragon Boat Festival best. It always in May or June.③ We eat zongzi in that day.④ We watch Dragon Boat Race. The race always is wonderful. ⑤

What a great country China is! If you want to go aboard, China will be you best choice.

（备注：下划线实线为已给句子，下划线虚线为有错误的句子。）

有错误的句子应修改为：

① It's a big country with a long history.

② My favorite festival is Spring Festival.

③ It is always in May or June.

④ We eat zongzi on that day.

⑤ The race is always wonderful.

从以上学生的作文可以看出，学生已经掌握了本节课的绝大部分内容。第一篇文章有两处小错误，而第二篇文章有三处小错误，但都不影响对文章的理解。

这两篇作文使我发现了存在的问题：

（1）学生在句子与句子、段落与段落之间没有用关系词，使得文章的整体性不够强。

（2）学生的文章中言语比较死板，句子比较平铺直叙。

从这些问题可以看出，以后教学努力的方向：

（1）注意句子与句子之间、段落与段落之间的联系，强调如何使用关联词，注重文章之间联系性。

（2）提供一些好词好句，鼓励优秀学生使用好词好句，争取拿满分作文。

此外，还是有一些疑惑。例如，现在的话题作文基本上都是遵循：单词——句子——写作这个顺序来展开的，如何创新话题教学呢？如何将课堂上得更加的生动，使学生更感兴趣呢？这一系列的问题还需要去寻找答案。

四、微课教学在话题复习中的注意事项

1. 注意课堂的完整性

要达到微课与话题复习的完美结合，我们就必须将微课和话题完美地结合在一起，起到画龙点睛的作用，否则就不能体现微课的作用，反而画蛇添足了。

2. 微课的设计是为话题复习服务的

为了更好地使学生有足够的输入，在进行读写综合前，前面的教学活动都是铺垫，微课也是如此。所以，在设计微课时要注意其作用，不能喧宾夺主。

总而言之，微课和话题复习的有效结合，既要突出微课"短小精悍"的特点，又要为话题复习提供足够的语言输入，为话题复习的最后输出做好充足的准备。

玩转英语课堂的微视频
——初中英语课堂微视频的设计与实施

初中话题写作微视频教学课例

一、课例背景

本课例是以优课 "Unit 2 I think that mooncakes are delicious！" 中的Section A Grammar focus 4a—4c为基础，重新设计了以 "The Spring Festival" 为主题的话题作文复习课。原课例是以 "中国文化" 为主题，介绍了中国的习俗和传统节日，最后谈论favorite festival。虽然原课例获得了部级优课，但存在着不足之处：①内容偏多不够细化。面面俱到，可往往面面都不到，重点不够突出。想把所有相关的中国文化的内容都讲到，但内容很空洞，主题不够突出；②主题内容想突出传承中华文化，但未突破。如何传承中国文化是我们升华的主题，在设计新的教学内容中，我们要着力解决这两个问题。

二、设计思路

（一）备课思维过程

本教学设计主要是解决部级优课中反思的两个问题。本教学设计是突出"中国文化"部分，但只抓住其中的一点展开即可。"the Spring Festival" 为教学主题是最具典型性的中国文化之精髓。这一主题范围小，以此展开教学主题突出，这就解决了第一个问题。文化要一代一代地传下去，每一代人要担当该代人的责任。"the Spring Festival" 是中国最传统、隆重的节日，传承这个传统文化是青少年必须承担的责任，这是对第二个问题的回答。

教师围绕文本设计出以学生为中心、激发学生综合动机、提高语言和思维能力的课堂。本节课的主要教学思路是了解春节的时间、活动和传统食物，分析讨论春节的意义，探讨如何传承中国文化。

（二）课堂教学活动

本节课的教学流程图如下图所示。

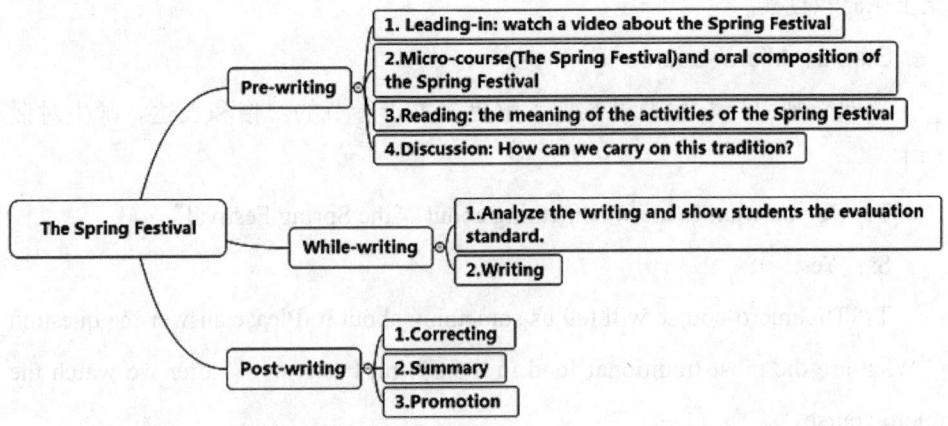

本节课中，授课者通过video，micro-course，reading，discussion这一系列的pre-writing 的活动为后面的writing做铺垫，由简到难，层层递进，不断地对学生进行语言输入，到最后产出。

三、教学过程

（一）Pre-writing

Step 1：Organization and leading-in

引入的内容是视频《春节是什么》，视频播放结束后，教师巧妙地将视频过渡到了课堂。导入与教学内容联系紧密，过渡自然。师生对话如下：

T：Good morning, boys and girls. Just now, we watched a video, could you please tell me what it is about?

Ss：The Spring Festival.

T：Yes. It's about "the Spring Festival". Today we are going to learn something about "the Spring Festival".

（Teacher leads to today's topic："the Spring Festival" and show the teaching aims.）

设计意图：春节是我国民间最隆重、最热闹的一个传统节日。视频《春节是什么》非常应景,将欢乐祥和的节日、亲人团聚、办年货、穿新衣,离家在外的孩子回家欢聚的欢乐氛围体现得淋漓尽致。通过这个视频内容,开门见山地引出本课话题,将学生带到了过春节的氛围中,既主题明确,又可以调动学生上课的积极性。

Step 2: Micro-course

授课老师引导学生通过微课了解更多关于春节的习俗和表达。师生对话如下:

T: Do you want to know something about "the Spring Festival"?

Ss: Yes.

T: The micro-course will tell us something about it. Please answer the question "What are the most traditional food in the Spring Festival?" after we watch the micro-course.

之后,教师呈现微课,并在微课后回到上面的问题。

教师在此环节中设计了口头作文: talk about something about the Spring Festival according to the micro-course and the mind-map(如下图所示),以说促写,为后面的写作做好铺垫。

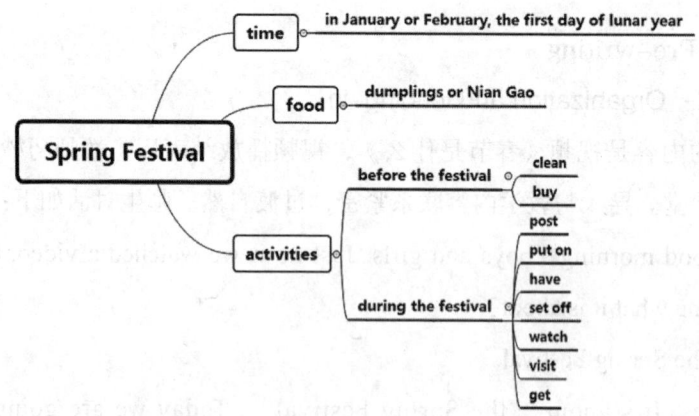

设计意图:学生对春节的时间、吃的传统食物、进行的活动比较熟悉,但缺乏知识的系统化。将这些内容以微课的形式呈现出来,设疑引入微课,将微课和上课的情景巧妙地联系到一起。通过微课了解春节的时间、活动和传统食物,依托思维导图和口头描述再现微课的内容,为接下来的写作积累语言素材。

Step 3: Reading

学生的口头作文中提到春节期间,中国人进行了很多活动。授课老师以此作为下一个环节的过渡,引导学生了解更多的关于春节的习俗。师生对话如下:

T: "The Spring Festival" is the most important traditional culture in China. Do you know why people do so many activities in "the Spring Festival"?

Ss: No.

T: Let's do some reading to find the answer and then finish the information card.

阅读内容如下所示:

The Spring Festival is the most important festival in China. In order to celebrate this festival, people do a lot of activities. Why do Chinese people celebrate it like that? This is because every activity stands for a certain meaning. Let's see what they stand for. (如下表所示)

Activities and meanings

Activities	Meanings
To clean the house	To clean away the poverty and bad luck.
To put on couplets ['kʌplits] (春联)	The words on couplets stand for people's good wishes and happiness for the new coming year.
To set off firecrackers (鞭炮)	To welcome the new year.
To Bai-nian (To visit friends and relatives)	To wish the old a healthy and long life.
To give lucky money to children	To wish the children spend the new year healthily and safely.

Food and meanings

Food	Meanings
Dumplings (饺子)	To get together, the shape of it means to bring fortune (财富).
Nian Gao (with the same sound of "年糕")	To get a higher income (收入) or a higher position.
New year's Eve dinner	Family reunion (聚会) dinner.

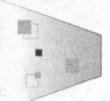

玩转英语课堂的微视频
——初中英语课堂微视频的设计与实施

信息归纳表所示：

Information card

1. The things that stand for people's good wishes and happiness.	
2. The activities to wish the old.	
3. The people who can get the lucky money.	
4. The food which means to bring fortune.	
5. The number of activities mentioned here.	

完成信息归纳后，根据阅读的表格进行分析和归纳出春节的含义。师生对话如下：

T：According to the reading material, can you tell me what "the Spring Festival" stands for?

Ss：It stands for the beginning of the new year.

T：What can the festival bring?

Ss：People think it can bring good luck, happiness, health, fortune, etc.

T：Yes. "the Spring Festival" means "new beginning and new hope" to Chinese. It can bring new hope to Chinese.

设计意图：中国人每年都过春节，为春节做准备，打扫卫生，买年货；春节期间放鞭炮、给亲朋好友拜年等，这些活动都是春节的传统活动，但学生不知道这一系列的活动的意义何在。通过阅读并完成信息归纳，了解春节各个习俗的含义，使学生对春节有更加深刻的印象。这在整个教学中起到了承上启下的作用。

Step 4：Video time

过春节意义深远，中国人都非常重视这个节日。很多中国人都会回到自己的故乡过节，为什么呢？播放不同的社会人员的采访视频。通过观看视频，讨论回家过春节的原因。师生对话如下：

T："The Spring Festival" is the most important time in the year. Who would you like to spend with at such an important time?

Ss：Families.

T: Where did you spend it with your family?

Ss: Hometown.

T: So did most Chinese people. Why? Let's watch a video to know the reason.

（Show students a video about "Go Home for the Spring Festival".）

（After watching the video）

T: Please discuss with your partner and tell the reason.

（After the discussion）

T: Why do Chinese people go home to celebrate the Spring Festival?

Ss: They want to spend "the Spring Festival" with their parents and brothers and sisters.

T: That's true. The Spring Festival is a good time for Chinese to spend time with friends and relatives. It can help to get closer.

设计意图：为了过春节这个隆重的节日，游子们想尽一切办法回家过年，为的就是和家人朋友团聚，联络感情。这个视频引起了在座的学生和老师的共鸣，是感情的升华，为接下来的写作积累了语言素材。

Step 5：Discussion

春节如此重要，作为青少年一代，我们有义务和责任将这个传统文化传承下去。但对于如何传承学生无从下手。为了使学生有话可说、有据可写，在这一环节里，教师展示了一些图片以供学生参考。教师的过渡语言如下：

T: So "the Spring Festival" is so important to us. We should carry on this tradition. How can we carry on this tradition? Please discuss with your group according to the pictures.

设计意图：中国传统文化博大精深、源远流长，身为中华儿女，中华文明的传承者，我们要承担起将中华民族传统文化发扬光大的历史责任。但如何传承，对初中生来说是无法用语言表达出来的。所以要引导学生借助图片，通过讨论了解如何传承传统文化，由此降低了这部分内容的难度，为接下来的写作积累了语言素材。

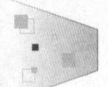

（二）While-writing

Step 1：Analyzing

前面的步骤已经为这篇话题作文做好了铺垫，积累了语言素材。学生的任务就是将本节课所学的知识运用到作文中。教师的过渡语言如下：

T：From what we have learned today, we know the Spring Festival well. Let's write a composition about it.

教师先组织学生分析作文，让学生知道写什么、怎么写。作文内容如下：

中国传统文化源远流长，春节是中国最重要的一个节日，请写一篇关于介绍春节的文章，内容包括：

（1）春节的基本介绍（time, food, activities）。

（2）过春节的重要意义所在（两点）。

（3）我们应该如何传承（carry on）传统文化（两点）？

Step 2：Writing

之后，学生有15分钟左右的时间进行写作。在学生写作期间，老师检查学生的写作，对他们出现的问题进行指导，并将他们的错误汇总。

设计意图：前面的每一个步骤都是为这个环节做准备的，层层递进，环环相扣，不断地输入，通过内化，最终达到输出的目的——以作文的形式产出。

（三）Post-writing

Step 1：Correcting

老师抽查一篇学生当场写的作文作为范文，与学生一起批改。之后让同组学生互改作文。改完后，教师在黑板上分析作文中的错误，并改正。

设计意图：分析学生的作文，通过边讲解边批改，让学生了解如何批改作文。同学之间交换作文互改，让学生欣赏同学的作文并且实践怎样修改作文。通过修改同学的作文并且改正错误的句子，让学生从同学的错误中预防自己犯同样的错误，从而达到优化作文的目的。

Step 2：Summary and promotion

写完作文后，老师组织学生进行总结并做主题升华。师生对话如下：

T：Now let's review what we have learned today. What do you know about the Spring Festival?

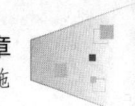

Ss：Yes. It's in...

T：Yes, you got it. China has a long history with great culture. We should be proud of being Chinese. As Chinese members ,we should carry on the essence of Chinese culture and chase any chance to promote（宣传）our country to the world.

设计意图：通过总结，让学生的脑海里再次呈现出这节课所学的内容，巩固所学的内容。在此基础上，主题升华，使学生热爱祖国，传承中国传统文化的精髓，实现正面的情感目标。

四、教学反思

本节课体现了以下几个方面的课堂设计理念。

1. 基于核心素养的话题作文的整体设计理念

语言是交流的工具，也是思想文化的载体，因此语言的人文性应得到与其工具性同等的重视。以学生为中心的课堂应帮助学生既提高语言能力，又提升思维品质。话题作文复习课教学设计应当使学生通过"运用所学语言知识与技能进行信息沟通、再现生活经历、描述周围事物、发表意见和观点的能力"。

授课老师以传承中国文化这条主线为引领，让学生从了解春节的基本活动、意义和如何传承进行了写作的pre-writing，while writing，post-writing三部曲。在微课之后，利用积累的素材，参考微视频，阅读图片内容，写一篇介绍中国文化的文章。这提高了学生的语言能力。

通过微视频、阅读、讨论等多样化活动进行思维延伸，让学生懂得从不同的角度看待问题、解决问题。通过讨论，了解春节游子回家过年的含义和如何传承中国的传统文化。这培养了学生的思维品质。

与此同时，让学生了解中国文化的重要性，了解中国文化的精髓并传承。这强化了学生的文化品格。

2. 引导学生深入了解中国文化，传承中国文化精髓

中国文化源远流长，中华民族的传统美德为我们的发展指明了方向。通过本节课，让学生更深刻地了解过年的寓意和春节对于中国人的意义，并引起学生的共鸣：我们一定要将这些文化传承下去。再由此引出怎样传承这一主旨，步步深入主题，把握核心思想。这些对学生而言，不仅是语言知识的输入，更是逻辑思维的输入。与此同时，也加强了爱国主义教育。

3. 贯彻立项课题，紧扣主题精神

本节课是我校市立项课题《初中英语微视频的设计与实施》的展示课。本节课的微视频有三个，导入部分的微视频《春节是什么》是直接从网上下载的，与主题"the Spring Festival"内容贴切，也体现了整节课的主旨；第二个微视频是自己制作的微课，主要介绍春节的时间、活动和传统食物；第三个视频是从网上下载后进行编辑的，视频的内容是家人期盼游子回家过年的场景。原视频是中文语音的，为了提升英语课的语言输入，授课者将其翻译并配上了英文音频。此微视频引起了在座的老师和学生的共鸣，这是感情的升华。通过微视频辅助作文课堂，增加了课堂的趣味性，提高了课堂效率。

五、课后评价

本节课授课老师合理地运用了微视频，对微视频通过制作调整，达到了运用的融合，培养了学生的核心素养价值观，集语言能力、思维品质、文化品格等于话题作文复习课中。本节课指向复习备考，对中考有着指导性作用。

六、不足之处

第三个视频"Go Home for the Spring Festival"引起了在座的老师和学生的共鸣，但由于学生讨论时间过短，效果不够强烈。整节课设计严谨，层层递进，但同时，学生自由发挥时间少，在培养思维品质方面有待加强。

一、东莞市初中英语微课设计脚本

1. 基本信息

基本信息

微课名称	写作微技能之段落展开策略：举例子和归纳	微课类型	写作微技能
授课/制作人	庄秋蚕	制作方式	录屏软件+PPT
适用对象	初三学生	时长	9分钟

续表

教学目标	通过学习本节微课，知道怎样对段落进行举例子和归纳
创新与亮点	1. 电话手表在学生中运用越来越普及，特别是5~12岁的学生。通过介绍热门的电话手表作为写作微技能的载体，电话手表有很多优点，本文介绍了它的优点，通过对比，引出"为什么"和"如何进行"举例子和归纳。最后通过练习，解除了家长的忧虑。 2. 通过对本节微课的学习，学生掌握了在文章中举例子和归纳的作用。 3. 介绍的内容贴近生活，图文并茂，内容丰富，简单易懂。

2. 设计与录制脚本

设计与录制脚本

教学步骤/活动	教学语言表述内容	多媒体配合方式与设计意图
Greeting & Learning goals	T: 欢迎进入东莞市英语微课堂，今天我们要学习的内容是写作微技能之段落展开策略：举例子和归纳。	多媒体配合方式： PPT 第1~2页。 设计意图： 组织课堂，老师和学生的上课准备。
Lead-in	T: First, I want to talk about two problems. The first problem-More and more students play phones in class. The second problem-Parents can't find their children easily, especially when they are in an emergency. How to solve the problems? Phone watches were invented in this situation. Phone watch is a kind of small phone which looks like a watch. Now more and more students especially aged from 5 to 12 have phone watches. Why? Phone watches have a lot of advantages. Firstly, it's very convenient for parents to know what is happening to the children. Secondly, it's very safe for children to use.	多媒体配合方式： PPT 第3~6页。 设计意图： 通过谈论电话引起学生的兴趣，并通过这个载体使学生进入到了本节课的教学。
Why & How	Teacher talks about the advantages about phone watches and then compares the one without examples and the one without examples. Students figure out the second one is better. And teacher explains why the second is better. After that teacher explains how to give examples and summarize in the our writing.	多媒体配合方式： PPT 第7~10页。 设计意图： 通过对比，使学生知道为什么和怎样在写作中举例子和归纳。

续表

教学步骤/活动	教学语言表述内容	多媒体配合方式与设计意图
Summary	Teacher summarizes what students have learned today.	多媒体配合方式：PPT 第11页。 设计意图：通过总结，让学生记住、巩固这节课所学的内容。
Exercise	Choose the best sentences.	多媒体配合方式：PPT 第12页。 设计意图：通过练习，巩固所学的内容。

二、"巧"用宾语从句，"美"化话题作文的微课教学设计方案

《"巧"用宾语从句，"美"化话题作文》微课教学设计方案

微课基本信息	知识点名称	"巧"用宾语从句，"美"化话题作文
	学科类型与教学对象	写作、初三学生
	预计上课时间长度	6分14秒

教学目标："巧"用宾语从句，"美"化话题作文。
教学资源与环境：PPT、电脑Windows XP以上系统、暴风影音。
教学过程： 1. 引入。介绍本节微课的主要内容。 2. 介绍为什么在话题作文中运用宾语从句。 3. 怎样在话题作文中运用宾语从句。 4. 总结。
设计理念与特色（微反思）： 1.《中国好声音》是学生最喜欢的娱乐节目之一，而周杰伦成为这届节目的导师则把这次节目推向了高潮，因为很多学生的偶像是周杰伦。李安是周杰伦的得意门生之一。选用了李安作为微课的主体内容，是比较能引起学生的兴趣的。 2.在第一次月考中，学生的作文写得很差，更不用说写出好词好句。而中考的评分标准则要求学生能够用好词好句。 3.学生刚刚学完宾语从句，设计如何将宾语从句运用到作文中可以温故而知新。
微课制作方式：CS软件+PPT录屏
专家点评：本节课通过mind-map、情境教学和启发式教学来讲本节微课内容，本节微课虽然只有6分多钟，但对初中学生如何将宾语从句运用到话题作文中帮助很大，温故而知新，内容丰富，简单易懂，这对初三学生的话题复习有很大的帮助。

三、优课课例1:"巧"用宾语从句,"美"化话题作文——中考话题作文训练

(一) Analysis of Students (学情分析)

They loved to watch the voice of China, one of the tutors is Jay Chou who was loved by the teenagers. And Tu Youyou has won the Noble Prize. That's the background of this lesson. The students have been in the junior school for more than two years. They have just known how to use the object clause, and they didn't do well in the first month test, especially the writing.

(二) Analysis of the Teaching Material (教材分析)

All the students have finished learning the object clause and they know how to talk about famous people.

(三) Teaching Goals (教学目标)

1. Target language

It's said that...

It's reported that...

It's known that...

It's believed that...

We know that...

We learn that...

I hope that...

I hope that I will...

I am sure that I will...

2. Ability goals

(1) To develop students' ability of listening and speaking skills.

(2) To foster students' abilities of communication and their innovation.

(3) Learn how to write a composition according to the instructions.

3. Strategy goals

Task-based approach (任务型教学法), Situational approach (情境教学法), The communicative language teaching (交际教学法).

4. Emotional goals

Learn to know more about Chinese culture and be proud of being a Chinese.

5. Teaching aid

A computer for multimedia use.（如下表所示）

（Teaching aid： A computer for multimedia use）

Teaching procedures

Steps	Teacher's activities	Students' activities	Ways
Step 1: Organization and Warming up	1. Organization: Organize the students by greeting.	Greeting.	组织课堂，老师和学生的上课准备。
	2. Let Ss watch a video about the Voice of China and lead to today's topic: talking about famous people.	Watch a video about the Voice of China and lead to today's topic: talking about famous people.	通过听歌曲引起学生的兴趣，并通过听歌曲使学生进入本节的课教学。
	3. Let Ss talk about Li An according to the mind-map.	Talk about Li An according to the mind-map.	利用思维导图了解李安，并将这些内容转化成宾语从句从而进入到本节课的中心内容。
	4. Show students the teaching aims about this lesson.	Learn about the teaching aims about this lesson.	了解本节课的教学目标。
Step 2: Presentation	Let students learn the micro-course.	Learn the micro-course.	通过学习微课，了解怎样描述人物，引入本节课的重点内容。
Step 3: Pre-writing	1. Let students guess who she is according to the picture.	Guess who she is according to the picture.	通过猜测引起学生的兴趣，并通过猜测使学生进入下一环节的内容。
	2. Let students watch some pictures about Tu Youyou and know something information about her according to the sentences.	Watch some pictures about Tu Youyou and know something information about her according to the sentences.	通过欣赏伴着音乐的图片和文字，了解屠呦呦的一些基本情况。

第五章 话题写作的微视频设计与实施

续表

Steps	Teacher's activities	Students' activities	Ways
Step 3: Pre-writing	3. Let students fill in the blank which is a passage about Tu Youyou.	Fill in the blank which is a passage about Tu Youyou.	通过短文填空，进一步了解屠呦呦的情况。
	4. Let students read the writing structures.	Read the writing structures.	通过阅读作文，使学生知道作文的基本要求。
	5. Let students analyze the first paragraph of the writing comparing with the micro-course.	Analyze the first paragraph of the writing comparing with the micro-course.	通过对比微课，使学生知道怎样写作文的首段。
	6. Let students analyze the second paragraph of the writing comparing with the micro-course.	Analyze the second paragraph of the writing comparing with the micro-course.	通过对比微课，使学生知道怎样写作文的第二段。
	7. Let students analyze the third paragraph of the writing comparing with the micro-course.	Analyze the third paragraph of the writing comparing with the micro-course.	通过对比微课，使学生知道怎样写作文的第三段。
Step 4: While-writing	Let the students write the composition according to what have learned today and use the object clause.	Write the composition according to what have learned today and use the object clause.	用本节课所学的知识写作文，并且学会运用宾语从句。
Step 5: After-writing	Check one of the students' writing and point out the mistakes.	Check one of the students' writing and point out the mistakes with the teacher.	一起修改一个学生的作文，指出错误。特别指出宾语从句的运用。
Step 6: Summary	Summarize what students have learned today.	Summarize the language points they have learned.	通过总结，让学生的脑海里再次呈现出这节课所学的内容，巩固所学的内容。

（四）课堂实录

Step 1: Organization and Warming up

T: Good morning, boys and girls. At the beginning of our lesson, I would like to watch a video, would you like to watch?

Ss：Yes.

（Teacher shows the video of Li An, and the students enjoy the video.）

T：Could you please tell me who the singer is?

S：Li An.

T：I want to know more about Li An.

（Teacher leads to talk about Li An according to the mind-map and then change them into the object clause.）

T：Today we are going to learn how to use the object clause properly and wisely in order to make our writing much better.

（Teacher leads to today's topic： how to use the object clause properly and wisely in order to make our writing much better and show the teaching aims.）

Step 2：Presentation

T：Do you know how to use the object clause properly and wisely in order to make our writing much better?

Ss：No.

T：The micro-course will tell you the answers.

（Teacher lets the students watch a micro-course about how to use the object clause properly and wisely in order to make our writing much better.）

（设计意图：通过学习微课，了解怎样描述人物，引入本节课的重点内容。）

Step 3：Before-writing

T：Just now, we know how to use the object clause properly and wisely in order to make our writing much better, later we are going to write a person, but first let's guess who she is.

（Teacher shows a picture about Tu Youyou which was taken when she was young.）

（Students don't know who she is, teacher shows more pictures about Tu Youyou and know something information about her according to the sentences.）

（设计意图：通过欣赏伴着音乐的图片和文字，了解屠呦呦的一些基本情况。）

(Teacher asks Ss to finish a passage about Tu Youyou.)

(设计意图：通过短文填空进一步了解屠呦呦的情况。)

(Finish the writing structures and analyze the important points one by one according the micro-course.)

(设计意图：通过阅读作文使学生知道作文的基本要求，对比微课，进行知识的迁移，使学生知道怎样写作文的每个自然段。)

Step 4：While-writing

T：From what we have learned today, we know something about Tu Youyou, let's write a composition about her.

(While students are writing, the teacher points out their mistakes.)

(Teacher checks one of the students' writing and points out the mistakes.)

(设计意图：用本节课所学的知识写作文，并且学会运用宾语从句。)

(设计意图：一起修改一个学生的作文，指出错误，特别指出宾语从句的运用。)

Step 5：Summary

T：Now let's review what we have learned today. What TV shows do you know?

(设计意图：教师和学生的最后总结让学生对自己今天学习的知识进行了梳理，又一次进行了强化，加深了印象。)

四、优课课例2：Chinese Culture中考话题作文训练

（一）Analysis of Students（学情分析）

The students have been in the junior school for more than two and a half years. They know some of the culture of China, such as the population, history, area, and traditional festivals, etc. They have mastered a lot of words and expressions about Chinese culture.

（二）Analysis of the Teaching Material（教材分析）

All the students have finished all the text book. And this topic is integrated with unit 7 in students' book for grade 8, book 2 and unit 2 and unit 10 in students' book for grade 9.

（三）Teaching Goals（教学目标）

1. Target language

Words：size, kilometers, country, population, place, festival, dumpling, custom, culture, chopsticks, celebrate, traditional

Phrases： shakes hands, for the first time, Spring Festival, Dragon Boat Festival, Mid-autumn Day, visit friends and relatives, get lucky money, watch Dragon Boat Race, watch the bright and full moon, a long history

2. Ability goals

（1）To develop students' ability of listening and speaking skills.

（2）To train students' ability of working in groups.

（3）To foster students' abilities of communication and their innovation.

（4）Learn how to write a composition according to the instructions.

3. Strategy goals

Task-based approach（任务型教学法）, Situational approach（情境教学法）, The communicative language teaching（交际教学法）.

4. Emotional goals

Learn to know more about Chinese culture and be proud of being a Chinese.

5. Teaching aid

A computer for multimedia use.（如下表所示）

（Teaching aid： A computer for multimedia use）

Teaching procedures

Steps	Teacher's activities	Students' activities	Ways
Step 1: Organization and Warming up	1. Organization: Organize the students by greeting.	Greeting.	组织课堂，老师和学生的上课准备。
	2.Let Ss play a guessing game about a map of China and lead to today's topic: Chinese Culture.	Play a guessing game about a map of China and lead to today's topic: Chinese Culture.	通过猜测引起学生的兴趣，并通过猜测使学生进入本节课的教学。
	3.Show students the teaching aims about this lesson.	Learn about the teaching aims about this lesson.	了解本节课的教学目标。

续表

Steps	Teacher's activities	Students' activities	Ways
Step 2: presentation	1. Let the students guess the answers of listening text.	Guess the answers of listening text.	通过猜测来检测学生是否了解中国的一些文化习俗，并且引入微课。
	2. Let students learn the micro-course.	Learn the micro-course.	通过学习微课，了解中国的一些传统的文化，引入本节课的重点内容。
	3. Let students check the answers of the listening text and review some of the customs and culture according to the micro-course.	Check the answers of the listening text and review some of the customs and culture according to the micro-course.	通过校对答案，将微课和本节课的内容联系在一起。
Step 3: Oral practice	1. Let students talk about something about China according to the micro-course.	Talk about something about China according to the micro-course.	根据微课学习的内容来谈论中国的基本情况，并且为后面的作文做好铺垫。
	2. Let students talk about something about favorite festival according to the micro-course.	Talk about something about favorite festival according to the micro-course.	根据微课学习的内容来谈论自己最喜欢的节日，并且为后面的作文做好铺垫。
Step 4: Writing	1. Let students analyze the composition.	Analyze the composition.	通过分析作文使学生知道怎样写作文。
	2. Let students write down the words and phrases they need for the composition.	Write down the words and phrases they need for the composition.	熟悉单词和短语，为写作文做好准备。
	3. Let the students know about the points they can get when they write down the main points.	Know about the points they can get when they write down the main points.	通过了解各个要点的分值，让学生更好地把握写作文的重点。
	4. Let the students write the composition according to what have learned today and use the good sentences in the slide.	Write the composition according to what have learned today and use the good sentences in the slide.	用本节课所学的知识写作文，并且学会运用好词好句。

续表

Steps	Teacher's activities	Students' activities	Ways
Step 4: Writing	5. Let students exchange their writings and check them.	Exchange their writings and check them.	交换作文互改，让学生欣赏同学的作文，并且了解怎样修改作文。
	6. Let students write down one or two sentences from the writing and correct them.	Write down one or two sentences from the writing and correct them.	通过修改同学的作文并且修改错误的句子，让学生从学生的错误中预防错误。
	7. Show students their correcting and check them.	Learn about the correcting.	检查学生修改错误的情况。
	8. Let students read the teacher's composition and explain it.	Read the teacher's composition.	分析老师的作文，突出老师运用了连词和过渡句，让学生多运用使文章更美。
Step 5: Summary	Summarize what students have learned today.	Summarize the language points they have learned.	通过总结，让学生的脑海里再次呈现出这节课所学的内容，巩固所学的内容。

（四）课堂实录

Step 1： Organization and Warming up

T： Good afternoon，boys and girls. At the beginning of our lesson, I would like to play a guessing game, would you like to play?

Ss：Yes.

（Teacher shows the map of China piece by piece, and lets students guess.）

T： Today we are going to learn something about China—Chinese culture.

（Teacher leads to today's topic： Chinese culture and show the teaching aims.）

Step 2： Presentation

T： Do you know something about Chinese culture?

Ss： Yes.

T: Let's guess the answers of listening text.

(Ss guess the answers.)

T: The micro-course will tell you the answers.

(Teacher lets the students watch a micro-course about Chinese culture and then check the answers of listening text.)

(设计意图：通过猜测来检测学生是否了解中国的一些文化习俗，并且引入微课。通过学习微课，了解中国的一些传统文化，引入本节课的重点内容。通过校对答案，将微课和本节课的内容联系在一起。)

T: Just now, we know something about Chinese culture, what else did the micro-course tell us?

Ss: History.

T: Yes. History. A…

Ss: A long history.

T: What else?

Ss: Population.

T: Yes, a largest population.

Ss: Size.

T: Good, the third largest country.

(Teacher asks Ss to pay attention to the verb "is" or "has" before them and then asks Ss to talk about something about some information about China.)

(设计意图：通过对微课的内容进行重现，让学生谈论中国的一些基本情况，为后面的作文做充分的准备。)

T: Besides some information about China, what else have we learned?

S: Traditional festivals.

(Teacher asks Ss to talk about their favorite festivals about China.)

(设计意图：通过对微课的内容进行重现，让学生谈论他们最喜欢的节日，为后面的作文做充分的准备。)

Step 4: Writing

T: From what we have learned today, we know that China becomes stronger and stronger, so more and more foreigners want to visit China, let's write a composition about China.

(Teacher asks Ss to analyze the composition. Teacher checks Ss if they have mastered the words and phrases they need and write down the words and phrases they don't master on a color card. Teacher sticks them on the blackboard in order to let students to use them when they are needed.)

(Teacher asks Ss to point out the points they can get by writing down the key points.)

(Teacher lets the students write the composition according to what have learned today and use the good sentences in the slide.)

(Teacher lets the students write down one or two sentences from the writing and correct them. Teacher shows students their correcting and check them.)

(Let students read the teacher's composition and explain it.)

(设计意图：学生梳理话题作文的单词和短语，为后面的作文做准备。通过了解各个要点的分值，让学生更好地把握写作文的重点。通过修改同学的作文并且修改错误的句子，让学生从其他同学的错误中预防错误。检查学生修改错误的情况。分析老师的作文，突出老师运用了连词和过渡句，让学生多运用使文章更美。)

Step 5：Summary

T：Now let's review what we have learned today. What TV shows do you know?

(设计意图：教师和学生的最后总结让学生对自己今天学习的知识进行了梳理，又一次进行了强化，加深了印象。)

五、优课课例3：基于微视频教学——微课的话题作文复习课

(一)教学材料

人教版《初中英语》九年级上册 Unit 2 I think that mooncakes are delicious，本单元涉及了"the Mid-autumn Festival"，所包含的内容有"中国文化"，由此设计了"the Spring Festival"这一节话题作文复习课.

(二)学情分析

本次授课对象九年级的学生，面临中考。他们的英语水平已经有了一定基础，在如何写出高水平的文章方面还需要不断的精细化练习。

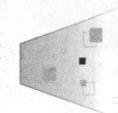

本课的话题"the Spring Festival",是同学们再熟悉不过的话题。本节课通过了解"the Spring Festival"的相关话题,并运用常用词汇、句型与表达结构,学生能写出与话题相关的简单的英语句子。但学生还需要更多思维能力的训练,学习如何阐述现象与观点、如何组织语言、整理思路,而后形成文章。

（三）教学目标

1. 语言能力

（1）通过同伴讨论、小组合作拓展思维、积累词汇和表达等素材。

（2）利用积累的素材,参考微视频内容,以平行写作的形式用简单的句子写一篇介绍中国文化的文章。

2. 思维品质

通过多样化的活动进行思维延伸,让学生懂得从不同的角度看待问题、解决问题,并结合自身经历提出合理的建议。通过讨论,了解春节游子回家过年的含义和如何传承中国的传统文化。

3. 文化品格

让学生了解中国文化的重要性,了解中国文化的精髓并传承。

学习能力：通过思维导图、同伴讨论、小组合作等方式,完成老师提出的各项小任务,并最终利用本课的知识完成写作任务。在教师的点拨和指导下,通过小组互评来修改自己的文章。

（四）教学设计理念

在二语习得的过程中,写作是一个长期的能力的积累过程。写作能力的提高需要大量输入,循序渐进,方法得当,教师在写作课堂中的角色尤为重要。本节写作课,我依照以下四个理论进行设计。

1. 过程性写作

其宗旨是以过程而非结果为中心,教学重点在于引导学生如何写,而不是仅聚焦于学生最后的作品。教学步骤大致可分为三个阶段——写前准备、写初稿、评价与修改。

2. 交际性写作

强调写作任务的交际性与真实性。学生的写作任务应该是生活中真实存在的,并且有真实的读者对象,以交际为目的,此外,要突出学生在写作活动中主体的地位，老师只是辅助，创设真实的交际情境和氛围，激发学生的写作欲望。

3. 任务型写作

以任务组织写作，在任务的完成过程中，以参与、体验、互动、交流、合作等方式，使学生发挥自身的认知能力，调动已有的语言资源，最终落实到写作的输出上。

4. 支架式写作

支架式写作，即搭建"脚手架"的写作，"支架"意为各种形式的帮助。它强调学生在教师的帮助下，主动探索，逐步解决问题，最终脱离老师帮助后独立完成写作任务。它包括四个方面，即情感支架、知识支架、活动支架、实践训练。情感支架要求教师通过各种方式激发学生的写作热情；知识支架要求教师帮助激活学生已有的背景知识和写作相关策略；活动支架要求教师将复杂问题拆解成梯度较小的几个小活动，鼓励和引导学生通过活动达到目标；实践训练要求教师通过实战训练帮助学生巩固和内化所学知识，能在拆除"脚手架"以后独立完成写作任务。

（Teaching aid：A computer for multimedia use）（如下表所示）

Teaching procedures

	Steps	Teacher's activities	Students' activities	Ways
Before-writing	Step 1: Organization and Warming up	1. Organization: Organize the students by greeting.	Greeting.	组织课堂，老师和学生的上课准备。
		2. Show students a video about "the Spring Festival Gala" and lead in today's topic "the Spring Festival".	Watch a video about "the Spring Festival Gala" and lead in today's topic "the Spring Festival".	引出本课话题，并让学生心中有目标有计划地紧跟课堂节奏，是任务型教学的体现。
		3. Show students the teaching aims about this lesson.	Learn about the teaching aims about this lesson.	了解本节课的教学目标。

续表

	Steps	Teacher's activities	Students' activities	Ways
Before-writing	Step 2: Micro-course	Show students a micro-course about the Spring Festival.	Watch a micro-course about the Spring Festival.	了解春节的时间、活动和传统食物，为接下来的写作积累语言素材。
		Let Ss talk about "the Spring Festival" with the partner according to the micro-course.	Talk about "the Spring Festival" with the partner.	复现春节的时间、活动和传统食物，为接下来的写作积累语言素材。
	Step 3: Reading	Let Ss do an information card to know why people do so many activities in "the Spring Festival".	Do an information card to know why people do so many activities in "the Spring Festival".	通过阅读完成信息归纳，了解春节习俗的含义。
	Step 4: Video time	Show students a video about "Go Home for the Spring Festival" and answer the question "Why do Chinese people go home to celebrate the Spring Festival".	Watch a video about "Go Home for the Spring Festival" and answer the question "Why do Chinese people go home to celebrate the Spring Festival".	观看视频，了解春节游子回家过年的含义，为接下来的写作积累语言素材。
		Let students discuss "What can you learn from the video" with the partner.	Discuss "What can you learn from the video" with the partner.	了解春节游子回家过年的含义，为接下来的写作积累语言素材。
	Step 5: Discussion	Show students some pictures and discuss "How can we carry on this tradition?" with the group.	Watch some pictures and discuss "How can we carry on this tradition?" with the group.	了解如何传承中国的传统文化，为接下来的写作积累语言素材。
While-writing	Step 6: Writing	Let students analyze the composition.	Analyze the composition.	通过分析作文，使学生知道怎样写作文。
		Let students write the composition.	Write the composition.	运用所学知识，完成本课的写作任务。

续表

	Steps	Teacher's activities	Students' activities	Ways
After-writing	Step 7: After-writing	Check one of the writings with the whole class.	Check one of the writings with the teacher.	分析学生的作文，了解如何批改作文。
		Let students exchange the writing with the partner and check it.	Exchange the writing with the partner and check it.	交换作文互改，让学生欣赏同学的作文，并且了解怎样修改作文。
		The teacher checks some of the mistakes the students made.	Check some of the mistakes they made with the teacher.	通过修改同学的作文并且修改错误的句子，让学生从学生的错误中预防错误。
	Step 8: Summary and Promotion	Summarize what students have learned today.	Summarize the language points they have learned.	通过总结，让学生的脑海里再次呈现出这节课所学的内容，巩固所学的内容。
		Call on students to love our country and carry on the essence of the traditional culture.	Call on to love our country and carry on the essence of the traditional culture	主题升华，使学生热爱祖国，传承中国传统文化的精髓，实现正面的情感目标。

（四）课堂实录

1.Before Writing

Step 1：Organization and Warming up

T：Good morning, boys and girls. Just now, we watched a video, could you please tell me what it is about?

Ss：It's about "the Spring Festival".

T：Yes. It's about "the Spring Festival". Today we are going to learn something about "the Spring Festival".

（Teacher leads to today's topic："the Spring Festival" and show the teaching aims.）

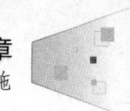

第五章 话题写作的微视频设计与实施

（设计意图：引出本课话题，并让学生心中有目标有计划地紧跟课堂节奏，是任务型教学的体现。）

Step 2：Micro-course

T：Do you know want to know something about "the Spring Festival"?

Ss：Yes.

T：The micro-course will tell something about "the Spring Festival". Please answer the question "What are the most traditional food in the Spring Festival?"

（Teacher lets the students watch a micro-course about "the Spring Festival" and then check the answer.）

（设计意图：通过设疑引入微课。了解春节的时间、活动和传统食物，为接下来的写作积累语言素材。通过校对答案，将微课和本节课的内容联系在一起。）

Step 3：Reading

T：Culture is a symbol of a nation. "The Spring Festival" is the most important traditional culture in China. Do you know why people do so many activities in "the Spring Festival"?

Ss：No.

T：Let's do some reading to know why people do so many activities in "the Spring Festival" and then finish the information card.

（After doing the information card）

T：According to the reading material, can you tell me what "the Spring Festival" stands for?

Ss："The Spring Festival" stands for the beginning of the new year.

T：According to the reading material, can you tell me what "the Spring Festival" can bring?

Ss：People think "the Spring Festival" can bring good luck, happiness, health, fortune, etc.

T：Yes. "the Spring Festival" means "new beginning and new hope" to Chinese. "The Spring Festival" can bring new hope to Chinese.

（设计意图：通过信息归纳，了解春节各个习俗的含义。）

Step 4：Video time

T：So people consider "the Spring Festival" as the most important time in the year. Who would you like to spend with at such an important time?

Ss：Families.

T：Where did you spend "the Spring Festival" with your family, your hometown or outside your hometown?

Ss：Hometown.

T：So did most Chinese people. Why do they go back to the hometown to celebrate the Spring Festival? Let's watch a video to know the reason.

（Show students a video about "Go Home for the Spring Festival" and answer the question "Why do Chinese people go home to celebrate the Spring Festival".）

（After watching the video）

T：Please discuss with your partner and answer the question "Why do Chinese people go home to celebrate the Spring Festival？"

（After the discussion）

T：Why do Chinese people go home to celebrate the Spring Festival?

Ss：They want to spend "the Spring Festival" with their parents and brothers and sisters.

T：That's true. The Spring Festival is a good time for Chinese to spend time with friends and relatives. It can help to get closer.

（设计意图：了解春节游子回家过年的含义，为接下来的写作积累语言素材。）

Step 5：Discussion

T：So "the Spring Festival" is so important to us. We should carry on this tradition. How can we carry on this tradition？Please discuss with your group according to the pictures．

（设计意图：了解如何传承中国的传统文化，为接下来的写作积累语言素材。)

2. While-writing

Step 6: Writing

T: From what we have learned today, we know that the Spring Festival. Let's write a composition about China.

Teacher asks Ss to analyze the composition.

While students are writing, the teacher collects their mistakes.

(设计意图：用本节课所学的知识写作文。)

3. After-writing

Teacher checks one of the students' writing and points out the mistakes.

Let students exchange the writing with the partner and check it.

The teacher checks some of the mistakes the students made.

(设计意图：分析学生的作文，了解如何批改作文。交换作文互改，让学生欣赏同学的作文并且了解怎样修改作文。通过修改同学的作文并且修改错误的句子，让学生从学生的错误中预防错误。)

Step 7: Summary and promotion

T: Now let's review what we have learned today. What TV shows do you know?

(Summarize what students have learned today.)

T: China has a long history with great culture. We should be proud of being Chinese. As Chinese members, we should carry on the essence of Chinese culture and chase any chance to promote（宣传）our country to the world.

(设计意图：通过总结，让学生的脑海里再次呈现出这节课所学的内容，巩固所学的内容。主题升华，使学生热爱祖国，传承中国传统文化的精髓，实现正面的情感目标。)

第六章 文化意识的微视频设计与实施

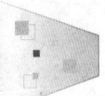
玩转英语课堂的微视频
——初中英语课堂微视频的设计与实施

有关文化意识培养的作文微视频教学设计

一、文化意识培养的必然性

众所周知,语言是社会的产物,是人类历史和文化的结晶。它凝聚着一个民族世代相传的社会意识、历史文化、风俗习惯等各方面人类社会所有的特征。不同的语言因其文化背景的不同,在使用上也存在着很大差异。《英语课程标准》中说:"使语言学习的过程成为学生形成积极的情感态度、主动思维和大胆实践、提高跨文化意识和形成自主学习能力的过程。""接触和了解英语国家的文化有利于对英语的理解和使用;有利于加深对本国文化的理解与认识;有利于培养世界意识;有利于形成跨文化交际能力。"中学英语教学是英语教学的初级阶段,是学习英语打基础的阶段,如果只重视语法、结构等语言知识的教学,而忽略跨文化意识的培养,势必会影响学生综合运用语言的能力。作为初中英语教师,我们应重视英语教学中文化知识的重要性,在教学中渗透文化知识,这对于培养学生综合运用英语的能力和进行跨文化交际的能力,对于提高英语教学质量具有十分重要的意义。

二、目前初中英语话题作文教学的现状分析

(一)教材分析

《义务教育英语课程标准》(2011年版)列出了 24 个基本话题,诸多话题构成了新课程教学内容的基本框架。我们所学的课文每个单元都有一个不同的话题,整个单元围绕着这个话题进行听说读写。按照每个教学单元,我们都进行了相关话题内容的学习。通过听、说、读各方面的训练,在单元学完后以

话题作文的形式进行输出，但此种写作都是以模仿偏多。学生可以模仿本单元前面的听力材料，对话和阅读进行写作，难度相对比较小，突出了工具性的教授，但缺乏创新，人文性被忽略，从而没有达到"立德树人"的根本任务。

（二）学情分析

由于初中英语的语言知识量非常有限，能力要求绝大多数也停留在英语语言的听、说、读、写上，而且为了考试，重在读和写，学生平时的学习很少涉及文化的内容，其对他们的考试成绩影响不大。

另外，英语只是诸多学习科目如语文、数学、物理、化学等中的一门学科，为了合理地分配各科时间，学生不可能花很多时间去学习语言所负载的文化，最多了解一下非常简单的与考试有关系的部分情景会话中涉及的一些礼貌用语、文化习俗。他们或许记单词、短语，背课文，做练习题都来不及呢！

由于上述原因，学生对中西方文化差异缺乏敏感性和洞察力，对富有文化内涵的语言现象理解不准确、不深刻，在运用英语进行跨文化交际时，学生往往按照汉语的文化习惯进行表达，从而表达不得体，甚至出现语用失误。

八年级是初中阶段的学生心理发展的关键期，是正值14~15岁的少年到青年的过渡阶段。他们好奇心重，有自己的看法、主张，希望得到认可，好动，冒险心态强，所以需要在教学设计的导入方面下功夫，借助多媒体手段，引起学生的兴趣。针对八年级学生的心理特点，需要将教学内容嵌入到具体的情境中，设计学生感兴趣的话题，进一步激发其学习英语的积极性。

八年级的学生开始有自己的想法和主张。根据这一特点，在英语教学的过程中，教师可以借助生动的视频激发学生的兴趣，学生的积极性得到调动后，自然会争先恐后地表达自己的观点。

所以，在教授英语的过程中，根据学生的个性特点、发展特征，适当地、及时地渗透背景文化知识，可以激发学生的学习热情，调动其学习的主观能动性，学生在潜移默化当中增强了其理解能力，使英语学习事半功倍。

三、初中英语作文微视频教学的意义

微视频在英语话题作文教学中具有培养学生的文化意识的意义。

微视频集声音、图像、文字于一体，可视性强、便于记忆，在英语教学

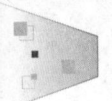
玩转英语课堂的微视频
——初中英语课堂微视频的设计与实施

中,它可以刺激学生的多重感官,使枯燥的教学过程变得生动、活泼,能够为学生创设逼真的教学情境;学习时间相对短,学生可以根据自身需求,制定学习计划,利用碎片式的时间进行学习,短时间内集中注意力,充分激发学习兴趣,提高自信心。教师通过微视频将知识简单化、多方位、多角度地向学生展示语言知识和背景文化,化虚为实,化静为动,提高他们的学习兴趣和理解能力;在直观性、趣味性、和富有感染力的情景下,通过观其形、辨其色、听其声、会其意、记其义、发其言等整体化地学习英语,学习中外优秀文化,从而拓展国际视野,理解和包容不同文化。

常见背景文化微视频的来源有以下几类。

1. 引用资源

直接引进相关的国外原声电影、电视片段、新闻等。

2. 修改资源

网络上相关的中英文小视频,通过后期制作,如修改为英文配音、英文字幕或中英相结合的教学微视频。

3. 自建微视频

教师自己通过相关的软件,如CS（Camtasia Studio）, Powerpoint 2013等,录制自己设计和演讲的微视频。现在多流行PPT录屏的微课、DV拍摄的小视频和原创flash动画。

本文将阐述如何在话题复习中渗透背景文化知识,促使学生更多地了解背景文化知识,从而提高跨文化意识,加深对英语的理解和应用。

四、初中英语话题作文教学文化意识培养的原则

文化意识在话题教学中的培养并不是盲目的,漫无目的的。我们在设计时必须遵循下列原则。

1. 以书为本的原则

教材是我们教学之根本。教材不仅是《课程标准》的代言人,更集中了众多专家、学者的专业智慧和学科水平,它是学科知识的精华、智慧的结晶。教材不是一般的材料、读物,它是根据教育目的和学生身心发展规律和认识特点,专门研制和编写的文本,适合相应特定阶段的学生学习。一切教学活动都

要紧扣教材进行。文化意识的培养要源于教材。

2. 以话题为纲的原则

《课程标准》倡导以话题为主线，围绕课程目标，并结合学情和教材特点进行立体、综合的教学设计与开发。话题成为设计的起点，围绕主题线索，进一步开发重构支撑话题的文本以引起学生的兴趣。文化意识的培养要基于话题。

3. 以文化为标的原则

《中学英语新课标》指出，接触和了解英语国家的文化有利于对英语的理解和运用，有利于加深对本国文化的理解与认识，有利于培养世界意识，有利于形成跨文化交际能力。然而，文化差异是跨文化交际的障碍，克服文化差异造成的交际障碍已成为整个世界共同面临的问题。语言教学中，向学生介绍异国文化知识并在实际教学中培养他们的文化意识，是理解和缩小文化差异的重要手段。

五、微视频在八年级话题写作教学中的文化意识培养的对策

对于八年级的学生，如何利用微视频教学，要使学生能够利用话题写作来培养文化意识。

本册教材每个单元都会专门有对写作的训练，其中每个单元Section B中的3c是写作训练。实际教学中，每周会有一节写作课对学生进行写作训练。例如八年级下册第一单元的话题是"health problems and accidents"，而本单元的写作是"make conversations between the school nurse and a student just had an accident or a health problem"。学生可以根据Section A 2d 的role-play和Section B 1a、1b和1c的内容进行模仿写作。这个写作内容比较简单，符合整个单元的教学主题，但缺乏创新性。根据本单元的话题设计一节与文化意识培养有关的话题写作课，具体内容（如下表所示）。

与文化意识培养有关的话题写作课设计

教学步骤/活动		活动设计	设计意图
Pre-writing	Step 1: Leading-in	观看一个关于的全国各地发生的多起溺水身亡的新闻微视频。	通过观看视频引出主题，发生突发情时如何面对。
	Step 2: Discussion	1. 谈论视频，抛出问题： （1）What happened? （2）How do you feel? （3）Why would the accident happened? 谈论并得出结论，并且由此以思维导图的形式引出表示feeling 的单词和accident 有哪些。 2. 从accident 的种类挑选出常见的四种：drowning accident, fire accident, car accident, health accident, 将学生分为四个组，各安排一个种类。	讨论视频引起大家的共鸣。通过讨论视频，复习相对应的单词和短语，为后面的写作活动做准备。
	Step 3: Reading	1. 日常生活中经常都有事故发生，阅读文章 "how to prevent the accidents"，并完成信息归纳。 2. 讨论文章的内容，发散学生的思维。	通过阅读文章，了解如何防止日常事故的发生。
	Step 4: Video time	1. 观看遇到不同的accident时候，如何施救的视频。 2. 根据视频讨论遇到上述accident 时应该怎样做。	通过视频作为输入，然后通过讨论的形式输出，为后面的写作做好准备。
While-writing	Step 1: Analyzing	1. 展示写作要求并做分析：在我们的日常生活中，各种事故频发。请你就此写一篇短文谈谈你的看法。 内容包括： （1）我们应该如何防止此类事故发生？（两点建议） （2）如果看到有人发生此类事故时，我们应该如何施救？ （3）呼吁同学们热爱生命，注意安全。 作文要求： （1）不能照抄原文。 （2）不得在作文中提到出现的学校真实姓名。	通过分析写作要求和给分标准，使学生知道如何将本篇文章写得更好。

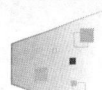

第六章 文化意识的微视频设计与实施

续表

教学步骤/活动		活动设计	设计意图
While-writing	Step 1: Analyzing	（3）语句连贯，词数80个左右。作文的开头已经给出，不计入总词数，也不必抄写在答题卡上。 2. 给出给分标准并做分析。	
	Step 2: Writing	15分钟左右的时间进行写作。在写作期间，老师检查学生的写作，对他们出现的问题进行指导。	前面的每一个步骤都是为这个环节做准备的，层层递进，环环相扣，不断地输入，通过内化，最终达到输出的目的——以作文的形式进行产出。
Post-writing	Step1: Correcting	1. 抽查其中一篇学生当场写的作文作为范文，与学生一起批改。 2. 同组学生互改作文。	分析学生的作文，通过边讲解边批改，让学生了解如何批改作文。同学之间交换作文互改，让学生欣赏同学的作文并且实践怎样修改作文。
	Step2: Summary and Promotion	组织学生进行总结，并做主题升华。	通过总结，让学生的脑海里再次呈现出这节课所学的内容，巩固所学的内容。在此基础上，主题升华，呼吁同学们热爱生命，注意安全，实现正面的情感目标。

本节课用了两个微视频。其中，第一个微视频是通过下载图片和剪辑新闻里的视频，再将自己录制好的相对应的英文解说词合并而成的视频。本微视频的内容贴近生活，通过将其内容改为英文解说的形式，不仅适合英语课程的要求，而且还强化了输入。第二个微视频是通过下载英文视频然后再剪辑而成的。此微视频由几个不同的视频剪辑而成，这些视频都是英语国家的本土视频，通过观看此视频，可以进一步了解西方文化，从而达到文化意识的培养。

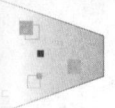

六、初中英语话题作文教学文化意识培养的建议

基于人教版2011新课标初中英语八年级下册话题作文教学的文化意识培养的设计建议，下面在go for it 八年级下册的教材中，将分单元介绍在话题作文教学中培养文化意识的建议。

话题作文教学中培养文化意识的建议

\multicolumn{3}{c}{八年级（下）}
Units	涉及的背景文化知识	话题作文写作建议
Unit 1 What's the matter	1. 西方国家的医疗系统，以及急救小常识。	在我们的日常生活中，各种事故频发。请你就此写一篇短文谈谈你的看法。内容包括： 1. 我们应该如何防止此类事故发生？（两点建议） 2. 如果看到有人发生此类事故时，我们应该如何施救？ 3. 呼吁同学们热爱生命，注意安全。 【文化意识链接】文化意识体现在"如果看到有人发生此类事故时，我们应该如何施救"中。
	2. 美国著名的探险家阿伦·罗尔斯顿和全球励志大师尼克·胡哲等的名人的生活态度，以及他们普世的价值观。	榜样教育对一个人的成长有很大的作用。China Daily 向大家征集关于榜样教育的文章。你最崇拜的名人是谁？请你介绍一下他（她），内容包括： 1. 介绍他（她）的一些生活经历。 2. 从他（她）的事例中，你学到了什么？你会为你的梦想怎样奋斗？ 3. 呼吁大家热爱生活，积极面对困难。 【文化意识链接】文化意识体现在介绍他（她）的一些生活经历中。
Unit 2 I'll help clean up the city parks	1. 志愿者文化的历史和发展以及在西方国家及我国的现状。	在我们的日常生活中，越来越多的人加入到了志愿者活动中。请你就此写一篇短文谈谈你的看法。内容包括： 1. 志愿者活动的现状和参加的意义是什么？ 2. 描述你自己参加志愿者活动的一次经历。 3. 呼吁同学们多参加志愿者活动，关爱他人。 【文化意识链接】文化意识体现在"志愿者活动的现状"中。

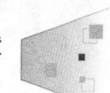

第六章
文化意识的微视频设计与实施

续表

八年级（下）		
Units	涉及的背景文化知识	话题作文写作建议
Unit 2 I'll help clean up the city parks.	2. 人与动物的和谐相处。	在我们的日常生活中，越来越多的人喜欢养宠物。请你就此写一篇短文谈谈你的看法。内容包括： 1. 描述人与动物相处的现状。 2. 描述你与动物和谐相处的事迹。 3. 呼吁保护动物，促进人与动物的和谐相处。 【文化意识链接】文化意识体现在"描述人与动物相处的现状"中。
Unit 3 Could you please clean your room?	欧美国家青少年关于做家务的态度，中西方国家的家长对待孩子做家务的态度。	很多人对于青少年做家务持不同的态度。请你就此写一篇短文谈谈你的看法。内容包括： 1 描述一下你家做家务的情况。 2. 你是支持还是反对做家务？请说明你的理由。（两点） 3. 呼吁大家做力所能及的事情，帮助家长。 【文化意识链接】文化意识体现在"你是支持还是反对做家务？请说明你的理由"中。
Unit 4 Why don't you talk to your parents?	1. 中西方家长对待孩子参加课外活动和课外学习班的态度以及做法。	为了孩子能够更加优秀，家长想尽一切办法让孩子参加课外活动。请你就此写一篇短文谈谈你的看法。内容包括： 1. 描述一下你父母对于参加课外辅导班的态度。 2. 你觉得应该参加还是不应该参加？请说明你的理由。（两点） 3. 呼吁合理安排休息时间，不能盲目参加课外辅导。 【文化意识链接】文化意识体现在"描述一下你父母对于参加课外辅导班的态度"中。
	2. 中西方国家培养孩子的态度和做法。	中西方国家对于培养小孩持不同看法。请你就此写一篇短文谈谈你的看法。内容包括： 1. 描述一下中西方国家培养小孩的态度和做法。 2. 你比较赞同哪种做法？请说明你的理由。（两点） 3. 呼吁大家不要宠溺小孩。 【文化意识链接】文化意识体现在"描述一下中西方国家培养小孩的态度和做法"中。
Unit 5 What were you doing when the rainstorm came?	介绍欧美国家一年四季的天气。	假如你是Kate,你的笔友张明今年暑假将来美国旅游，请你介绍一下美国的情况，内容包括： 1. 美国的天气情况和饮食情况。 2. 美国的名胜古迹。 3. 希望他在美国玩得开心。 【文化意识链接】文化意识体现在"美国的天气情况"中。

149

续表

Units	涉及的背景文化知识	话题作文写作建议
八年级（下）		
Unit 6 An old man tried to move the mountains.	中国民间神话传说和西方童话故事。	学校的读书节就要来了，学校广播站向大家征集关于课外阅读的文章。内容包括： 1. 介绍一下你平时的读书情况。 2. 简单介绍你最喜欢的一个中国民间神话传说或西方神话故事，并说明你喜欢这个故事的原因。（两点） 3. 呼吁大家多读书。 【文化意识链接】文化意识体现在"简单介绍你最喜欢的一个中国民间神话传说或西方神话故事"中。
Unit 7 What's the highest mountain in the world?	1. 了解我国和世界的一些"自然地理之最"中的知识。 2. 了解我国明长城的基本知识。 3. 了解珠穆朗玛峰及人类克服困难、挑战极限的精神。 4. 了解国宝大熊猫及动物保护。	越来越多人喜欢到中国旅游，作为中国人，我们很自豪，请根据下面的提示写一篇介绍中国的文章，欢迎外国朋友到中国。内容包括： 1. 中国的基本介绍，如饮食，天气等。 2. 中国的名胜古迹介绍。 3. 欢迎大家来中国旅游。 【文化意识链接】文化意识体现在"中国的名胜古迹介绍"中。
Unit 8 Have you read Treasure Island yet?	1. 初步了解经典英美文学作品，如《小妇人》《鲁滨逊漂流记》《金银岛》《汤姆索亚历险记》等。 2. 了解西方流行乐队文化以及美国乡村音乐。	学校兴起了欣赏英美文学作品的热潮，请你就此写一篇书评。内容包括： 1. 简单介绍你最喜欢的一部英美文学作品的主要内容。 2. 说明你喜欢这部作品的原因。 3. 呼吁大家多读书。 【文化意识链接】文化意识体现在"简单介绍你最喜欢的一部英美文学作品的主要内容"中。 你喜欢音乐吗？请你谈谈对音乐的看法。内容包括： 1. 介绍你最喜欢的音乐类型和代表人物。 2. 音乐对你生活的影响。 3. 呼吁大家享受音乐，热爱生活。 【文化意识链接】文化意识体现在"介绍你最喜欢的音乐类型和代表人物"中。

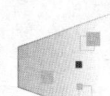

续 表

八年级（下）		
Units	涉及的背景文化知识	话题作文写作建议
Unit 9 Have you ever been to a museum?	1. 了解各类博物馆、主题公园和名胜古迹。2. 了解新加坡的语言、食物、气候的特色。	你最喜欢的地方在哪里？请你写一篇文章简单介绍你去过的一个地方。内容包括： 1. 介绍这个地方的基本情况：地理位置，人口，语言，气候等。 2. 介绍你参观的名胜古迹。 3. 希望再次在此游玩。 【文化意识链接】文化意识体现在： 1. 介绍这个地方的基本情况：地理位置，人口，语言，气候等。 2. 介绍你参观的名胜古迹中。
Unit 10 I've had this bike for three years.	1. 国外的庭院售卖、慈善捐赠活动。	合理处理可回收物品有助于保护环境。请你简单介绍你平时怎么处理可回收物品。内容包括： 1. 简单介绍国外的庭院售卖、慈善捐赠活动的概况。 2. 介绍你平时怎么处理可回收物品。 3. 呼吁大家保护环境，合理处理可回收物品。 【文化意识链接】文化意识体现在"简单介绍国外的庭院售卖和慈善捐赠活动的概况"中。
	2. 我国乡村生活的变迁。	随着中国人民生活水平的不断提高，中国农村发生了巨大的变化。请你就此写一篇短文谈谈你的看法。内容包括： 1. 简单介绍你家乡10年前的情况。 2. 你家乡现在的情况。 3. 呼吁大家多回家乡看看。 【文化意识链接】文化意识体现在"①简单介绍你家乡10年前的情况，②你家乡现在的情况"中。

七、基于微视频教学的学生调查问卷分析

微视频教学的学生调查问卷旨在了解运用微视频进行教学后，学生的学习兴趣以及在写作方面学习效果的变化。通过学生的评价，可以真实地反映运用微视频进行英语教学后的效果。调查问卷发出97份，收回93份，有效率为95.9%，问卷采用不记名的方式作答，内容涉及个人基本情况、学习兴趣、写作学习、效果评价等。数据统计选择的工具是Excel。教学问卷及统计结果分析如下。

玩转英语课堂的微视频
——初中英语课堂微视频的设计与实施

1. 你对利用微视频辅助英语教学感兴趣吗？

  A. 非常感兴趣   B. 比较感兴趣

  C. 一般   D. 不感兴趣

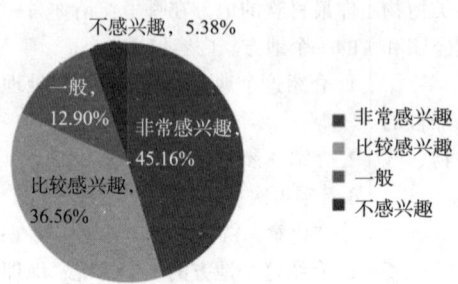

问卷数据显示，对于利用微视频辅助英语教学的总体看法是，45.16%的学生对利用微视频辅助英语教学非常感兴趣，36.56%的学生对利用微视频辅助英语教学比较感兴趣，12.90%的学生认为一般，只有5.38%的学生对在教学中使用微视频不感兴趣。这表明和传统教学方式相比，绝大多数学生对微视频教学持积极态度，说明在英语教学中使用微视频对提高学生学习英语的兴趣是有帮助的。

2. 你认为微视频对促进写作教学和文化意识的了解效果如何？

本学期对在话题写作教学上运用微视频的效果进行了调查问卷，学生问卷结果如下表所示。

微视频对促进听、说、读、写教学方面的效果

	非常有帮助（人）	较大帮助（人）	一点帮助（人）	没有帮助（人）
1. 调动多种学习器官，提高了学习效率	37	32	16	8
2. 对本节课所学的英语进行交流的情况	36	34	16	7
3. 对英美文化差异的理解情况	40	35	17	1
4. 帮助本节课写作能力的提升情况	39	30	20	4

调查结果表明，采用微视频教学能从听觉、视觉及想象力等方面，帮助学生学习英语，同时说明，英语课堂能调动学生的视觉、听觉等感官，更能激发

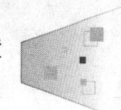

学生的学习兴趣，能提高学生的交流热情。微视频教学还可以帮助学生加深对英美文化的理解，为写作能力的提升提供了更加有效的途径。

八、结语

微视频是初中英语一个生动有趣且行之有效的学习新手段，将中西方文化背景知识通过微视频融入话题写作教学中，改变了传统的英语教学模式与方法，能够激发学生学习英语的兴趣，同时能给学生提供更多的相关知识，开阔学生的视野，培养学生的创新思维。将微视频融入平时的课堂教学中，一学期下来，学生的课堂表现明显改善，学习态度明显转变，学习兴趣有所提高，写作水平也有了一定程度的提高。但写作水平的提高是一个比较漫长的过程，不是短时间能达成的，需要不断探索。

初中文化意识培养的微视频教学实施

一、教学背景

（一）文化意识培养的重要性和途径

美国跨文化交际学家Samovar曾说："语言背后是有东西的，而且语言不能离开文化而存在。"2011年，我国教育部颁布实施了《英语课程标准》（以下简称《标准》），以语言技能、语言知识、情感态度、学习策略和文化意识五个方面共同构成英语课程总目标。文化意识包含了四个方面，即文化知识、文化理解、跨文化交际意识和能力。其中，在文化意识的分级目标中提出，在学习英语的过程中，接触和了解外国文化有益于对英语的理解和使用，有益于加深对中华民族优秀传统文化的认识与热爱，有益于接受属于全人类先进文化的熏陶，有益于培养国际意识。

文化意识培养的最终目的是提高跨文化交际能力，这是一个缓慢而长期的过程，而课堂教学是教师传授知识的主要手段也是培养学生文化意识的主阵地。文化意识的培养离不开文化教学，文化意识培养成败的一个重要指标就是文化教学的实施效果。这里所谓的文化教学，主要是从知识、态度、能力三方面进行的，它的教学重心是培养学生的跨文化交际意识和能力。课堂教学对学生跨文化意识培养主要是通过词汇、阅读、基础语法、文化、写作等教学课程实现的。

（二）文化意识与国际理解的关系

1947年，教科文组织将国际理解的核心观念确定为理解国际重大问题、尊重联合国和国际关系、消除国际冲突的根源、发展对他国的友好印象。这体现了国际理解教育立足于民族、国家和文化差异而通过教育消除隔阂、促进共存、维护和平的特点。

《标准》强调，外语的学习应该有利于学生认识世界的多样性，在体验中外文化的异同中形成跨文化意识。《标准》明确表明，教师在教学中要意识到语言学习有丰富的文化内涵和背景，注重培养学生的文化意识，增进国际理解。

在《标准》的分级目标之情感态度目标及文化意识目标中还明确提出，学生要乐于接触外国文化，增强爱国意识，对祖国文化有更深刻的了解，具有初步的国际理解意识；要培养学生的合作精神，拓展学生的国际视野，提高学生对中外文化的敏感性和鉴别能力，进而提高学生的跨文化交际意识和交际能力。

由此可见，文化意识和国际理解是相辅相成、息息相关的。而初中年龄段，正是学生正确世界观形成的初步阶段，教师应该充分挖掘教学资源，在进行语言知识传授的同时进行文化意识培养，提升学生的国际理解意识。

二、教学分析

（一）教学内容

本节课的内容为自编内容。《标准》附录5所列的话题项目表共24项，教师所在学校初三中考话题复习基本是围绕这些话题来复习的。其中第14项是安全和救护，根据这一话题，教师在进行中考话题复习时，结合国际时事，设计了一节以美国袭击叙利亚为背景，以"Help them, they want peace!"为主题的读写课，通过让学生了解战争对儿童的伤害以及战争中国家的儿童对和平的渴望，提高学生对国际事件的鉴别能力，从而提高国际理解意识。针对读写课以读促写的原则，教师自编了一篇302字的阅读材料，生词率为3%，难易度适中；自编了一篇书面表达题，设置了描述现状、看法和建议以及呼吁三个维度的写作，符合本地中考阅读篇章和写作的设置要求。

（二）学情分析

上课学生为九年级的学生，本节课设计于中考复习的第三轮复习：话题复习。本节课的主题是基于国际事件的安全与救护，学生对叙利亚的背景有初步的认识,但对战争中孩子的现状了解得不多,让学生写出对战争的看法和建议,是有一定难度的。

(三)教学设计

教学设计思路如下图所示。

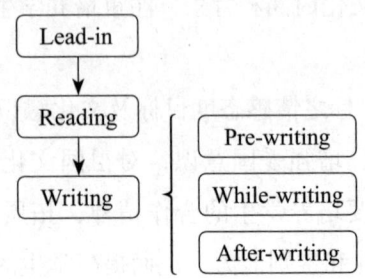

三、教学实施

(一)教学过程设计

Step 1:Lead-in

播放介绍叙利亚的视频给学生看,随之向学生提问,通过问题"Do you know Syria? Where is Syria? What's the capital of Syria?"检测学生对叙利亚的了解,其中第三个问题如果学生关注国际时事,一定知道大马士革这个首都。

设计意图:视频导入形象生动,给学生提供接触外国文化的机会,让学生在欣赏美景的同时引出话题,唤醒学生的元认知,拓展学生的视野,提高学生对中外文化异同的敏感性和鉴别能力。在引出问题的同时,借助问题设疑为下一步的阅读埋下伏笔,也为学生追求美好事物的情感态度做铺垫。

Step 2:Reading

引出话题之后,引导学生进行阅读文章。文章的内容是关于叙利亚的简介,包括其历史、位置、语言、民族、中叙关系以及国家现状,学生在进行阅读时填写以下信息卡(如下图所示)。

第六章
文化意识的微视频设计与实施

Information card

1. The full name of Syria	The Syria Arab Republic
2. The location of Syria	Western Asia
3 The name that Damascus known as	The city of heaven
4 The location of Damascus	Southwest of Syria
5 The time of the civll war in Syria	8 years

设计意图：本设计在培养学生阅读能力的同时，也给学生提供了相关的背景知识，对学生进行文化知识渗透，以期达到文化理解。文章的最后点明了叙利亚处于长达8年之久战争现状和孩子们对和平的渴望，为下一步的叙利亚战前战后对比埋下伏笔。

Step 3：Writing

（1）Pre-writing

① 通过视频和图片，配以文字和教师解说，让学生了解战争前后的叙利亚：建筑被毁，人们无法正常生活、学校和家园被毁，孩子流离失所（如下图所示）。

157

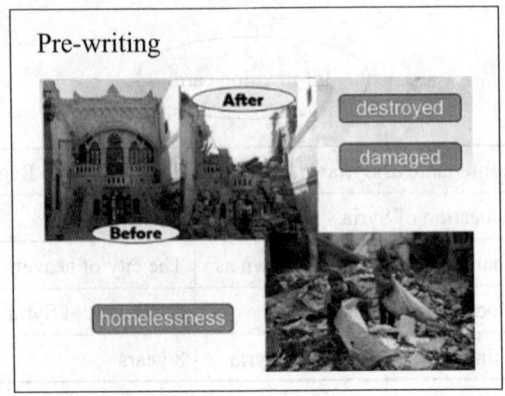

Teacher: The Syrian civil war began in 2011. It has lasted 8 years. Because of the war, there used to be old buildings, but now they are destroyed. The schools are damaged. Where are the children? They can't go to school. They have no home, no families and they are always hungry!

设计意图：在阅读前进行语言知识和背景知识的输入，为写作做铺垫。同时，让学生更直观地了解战争后的国家状况，引发学生情感的投入，提升学生对国际事件的鉴别能力。

② 阅读叙利亚9岁女孩Bana的网上留言截图（如下图所示），标注留言中的关键词，引导学生了解战争中孩子的境况和渴望。

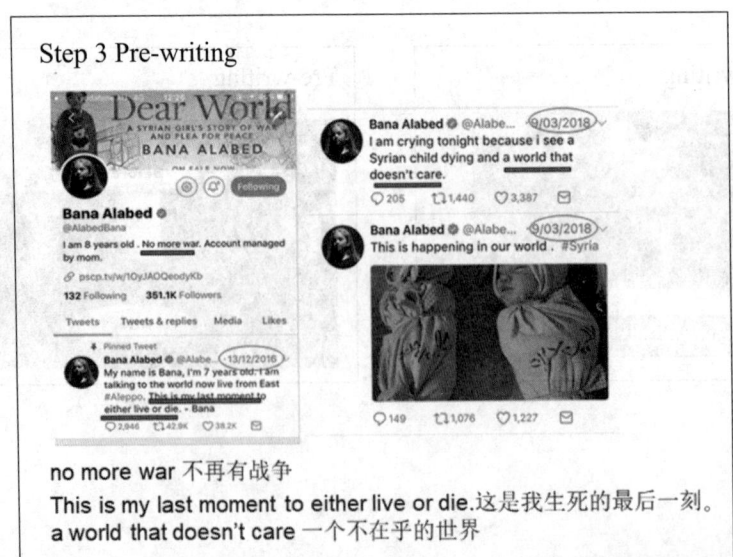

第六章
文化意识的微视频设计与实施

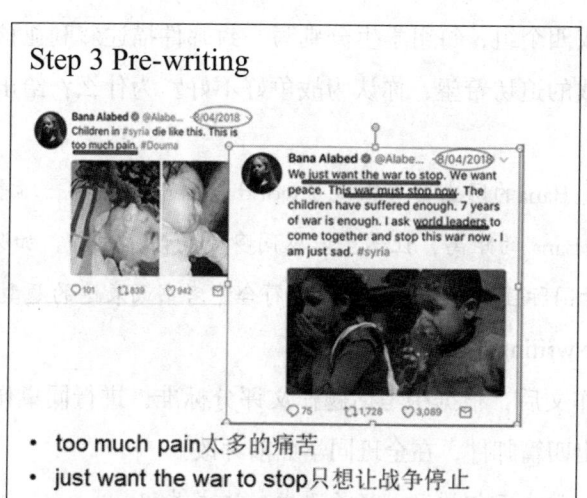

设计意图：从孩子的角度来理解战争的残酷和战争中孩子对和平的渴望，引起学生的共鸣，诱发学生的同情心和想帮助这些孩子的强烈愿望。标注重点词汇，目的是为写作做词汇的铺垫。

③ 微博留言。两人一组，给叙利亚的孩子在微博上留言2～3句话，告诉他们该如何自我保护（如下图所示）。

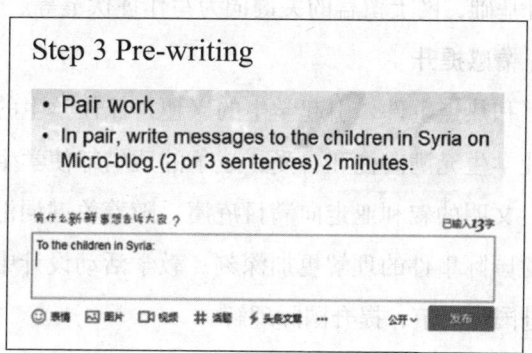

设计意图：结合中考话题设计活动，给国际孩子提供帮助，增进学生的国际友谊，提升国际理解意识。

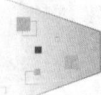

玩转英语课堂的微视频
——初中英语课堂微视频的设计与实施

（2）While-writing

把学生分成四个组，每组学生分别写一封邮件描述叙利亚孩子的现状，表达孩子渴望停战的迫切希望，你认为战争好不好？为什么？给出两点建议，呼吁世界和平。

设计意图：Bana的网上留言出现了world leaders的字样，顺着Bana的话写邮件，拉近学生与Bana的距离，让学生以感同身受的情感写作，加深学生对国际事件的理解，提升国际理解意识。写作设计符合中考书面表达的题型，直击中考。

（3）After-writing

学生写完作文后，根据中考话题作文评分标准，进行同桌作文互评，然后教师抽查，选出四篇邮件，在全班同学面前评改。

设计意图：学生互相学习，扬长避短，达成共识。

（二）教学反思

本节课通过在九年级班级试讲，结合学生课堂反馈和听课教师的意见，我又进行了深刻的反思，认为本节课有以下几点做得比较好。

1. 巧妙引导，环环相扣

作为课堂的引导者，教师通过视频、图片、网上留言等方式步步为营，每一个设计都为下一个活动打基础，做铺垫，使看似毫无相关的活动紧密相连，如阅读文章为下一步的描述叙利亚的战前、战后埋伏笔，写作前的语言输入和情感态度为写作打基础，网上留言的关键词为写作埋伏笔等。

2. 抓住关键，情感提升

通过关键词汇和热点事件，引起学生的兴趣，抓住学生的情感变化。美丽战争前的叙利亚让学生充满向往和喜爱，战争的残酷却使学生心情沉重，教师带着学生从古老、文明的叙利亚走向满目疮痍，随着关键词汇的输入，学生的心情跌宕起伏，对国际事件的理解更加深刻；教学活动设计中，有同龄人之间的互动设计，增进国际友谊，提升国际理解。

3. 文化培养，思维碰撞

本节课不仅让学生了解了中外文化的差异，了解了和平年代战争中国家的境况，也大胆地让学生参与并为世界和平而努力。学生可以有不同的建议，这是对学生创造性思维的培养，而教师在全班同学面前评改四篇作文，是让学生

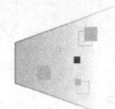

进行批评和自我批评，进行思维的碰撞。

本节课存在的主要问题是课堂输入信息量不足。由于初中生对国际事件理解的局限性，学生对叙利亚的了解仅来自本节课的一篇阅读和一些视频图片，导致学生的作文产出甚少有新颖的、有建设性的内容，这是由初中学的年龄特点导致的，也是我们日常教学中应该关注的方面。

（三）教学评析

这是一节典型的中考话题读写课，赋予了文化的因素。从对本课的分析中，我们可以看到：①文化意识话题的教学材料是可挖掘的，不应局限于课本教材；②文化意识的培养在教学中是可实施、应鼓励的；③学生的国际理解意识是可持续的、多渠道的发展。因此，作为英语教师，我们在英语教学中，充分挖掘教学资源，让学生接触和了解外国文化有益于对英语的理解和使用，有益于加深对中华民族优秀传统文化的认识与热爱，有益于接受属于全人类先进文化的熏陶，有益于培养国际意识。

一、文化案例文章赏析

The Syrian Arab Republic, short for Syria, lies in western Asia. Syria has an area of 185,180 square kilometers. It is a country with a long history and ancient civilization（文明）. And Syria is famous for its natural scenes, humanity（人文）and historic sites（历史遗迹）. The Syrian capital Damascus is known as the city of heaven. It is in southwest of Syria. It is a beautiful city with a history of 4500 years. It's one of the oldest inhabited cities in human history. In 1986, UNESCO（联合国教科文组织）added it on the list of World Heritage（世界遗产）.It has a population of more than 4.71 million in 2009.

The Syrian flag has three shades of red, white and black, meaning that it once joined the United Arab Republic. The Syrian official language is Arabic. English and French are spoken there, too.

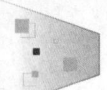

二、微课教学设计方案举例（如下表所示）

《Unit 6 Dragon Boat Festival》微课教学设计方案

微课基本信息	知识点名称	Dragon Boat Festival
	学科类型与教学对象	文化专题、初一学生
	预计上课时间长度	10分钟

教学目标：To know about the Dragon Boat Festival and the boat races.

教学资源与环境：PPT、电脑Windows XP系统、暴风影音播放器。

教学过程：本节微课的主题是端午节的习俗和龙舟赛。首先以沙画视频引入端午节的来历，然后对端午节的时间、传说人物、传统食物和传统活动进行介绍，介绍之后用一段英文进行描述，以让学生对端午节有一个全面的认识；接着通过一段赛龙舟的视频介绍龙舟赛这个活动的一些基本规则。最后总结本节课的学习内容。

设计理念与特色（微反思）：
1. 本节微课以沙画的视频引入，介绍端午节的来历，能够引起学生的兴趣。
2. 在介绍龙舟赛时，插入了一小段赛龙舟的视频，让学生更直观地了解龙舟赛。

微课制作方式：CS软件+PPT录屏

专家点评：本节微课沙画是一个亮点，通过沙画的形式把端午节的由来呈现了出来。而第二个亮点是赛龙舟的视频。整节微课语言简洁易懂，图文并茂，非常适合初一学生的年龄特点和知识水平。

《Chinese Culture》文化背景介绍的微课教学设计方案

微课基本信息	知识点名称	《Chinese Culture》文化背景介绍
	学科类型与教学对象	文化专题、九年级学生
	预计上课时间长度	9分钟

教学目标：结合初中所学的内容，了解中国文化背景。

教学资源与环境：PPT、电脑Windows XP以上系统、暴风影音。

教学过程：
1. 引入本节微课的主要内容。
2. 中国基本情况介绍。简单介绍中国的面积、人口和历史。
3. 中国习俗的介绍。简单介绍中国的两个习俗，初次见面时握手和用筷子吃饭。
4. 中国节日的介绍。重点介绍中国的三个节日：春节、端午节和中秋节。
5. 总结。

续表

设计理念与特色（微反思）：
根据《go for it》的教材进行整合，把八年级下册unit 7和九年级unit 2、unit 10等的内容整合成了Chinese Culture这个文化背景的微课，为了学生更好地了解自己的国家，并且通过学习本节微课知道怎样用英文来介绍中国。本节课通过mind-map、情境教学和启发式教学来讲本节微课内容，中国的面积、人口和历史，中国的两个习俗，初次见面时握手和用筷子吃饭，中国的三个节日：春节、端午节和中秋节等这些都是学生熟悉的课本知识。通过学习本节微课，学生可以对所学的内容温故而知新。
微课制作方式：CS软件+PPT录屏。
专家点评：
本节课通过mind-map、情境教学和启发式教学来讲本节微课内容，本节微课虽然只有9分多钟，但对初中所学过的中国文化的知识进行整合和汇总，温故而知新，内容丰富，简单易懂，这对于九年级学生的语法复习有很大的帮助。

《Unit 10 You're supposed to shake hands》文化背景介绍的微课教学设计方案

微课基本信息	知识点名称	《You're supposed to shake hands》文化背景介绍
	学科类型与教学对象	文化专题、九年级学生
	预计上课时间长度	7分28秒

教学目标：结合unit 10的语法点be supposed to do，了解英国国宴的餐饮文化背景。
教学资源与环境：PPT、电脑Windows XP以上系统、暴风影音。
教学过程：   1. 以英国国宴的视频引入本节微课，介绍本节微课的主要内容。   2. 对英国国宴的礼遇、穿着、礼仪、谈、吃等基本情况进行介绍。   3. 总结。
设计理念与特色（微反思）：   1. 本节微课以英国国宴的视频引入，介绍英国国宴的来历，引起学生的兴趣。   2. 在介绍英国国宴时，图文并茂，让学生更直观地了解英国国宴。
微课制作方式：CS软件+PPT录屏。
专家点评：   本节微课通过视频的形式把国宴的由来呈现了出来。而第二个亮点是图文并茂介绍英国国宴。整节微课语言都围绕着句型：be supposed to do sth.来展开，简洁易懂，生动有趣，内容丰富，这对于九年级学生的语法复习有很大的帮助。

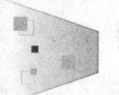

玩转英语课堂的微视频
——初中英语课堂微视频的设计与实施

《Unit 4 The Pop Music in England》微课教学设计方案

微课基本信息	知识点名称	Unit 4 The Pop Music in England
	学科类型与教学对象	文化专题、九年级学生
	预计上课时间长度	10分钟

教学目标：让学生了解英国乐队the Beatles，进一步让学生对英语歌感兴趣。

教学资源与环境：CS软件，PPT，电脑Windows XP，PPTV播放器，格式工厂。

教学过程：
第一，由本单元的人物Candy做引入，听两段the Beatles演唱的经典歌曲《Hey, Jude》和《Let It Be》，让学生初步知道the Beatles并激发学生了解这个乐队。第二，播放一段新闻，让学生知道虽然the Beatles已经有超过50年的历史，但世界各国的很多人还是很喜欢这个乐队。第三，具体地介绍the Beatles。第四，欣赏这个乐队的成员Paul McCartney在2012伦敦奥运会上演唱《Hey, Jude》的视频。

设计理念与特色（微反思）：
Unit 4关于文化的背景很难确定，最后根据其中一篇关于歌手Candy的文章而想到可以让学生了解英国的音乐。而谈到英国的音乐，不得不说的就是甲壳虫乐队了。因为它对英国的文化产生了非常大的影响。这个乐队对于现在的中国中学生来说可能太老旧了，所以笔者首先用微信的形式引入，让学生先听音乐，再让学生通过新闻了解这个乐队在全球已经风靡了50多年，以激发学生的兴趣，最后播放乐队的成员Paul McCartney在2012伦敦奥运会上演唱《Hey, Jude》的视频，使大家感受到这个乐队是多么有影响力，从而对它的歌曲感兴趣。

微课制作方式：CS软件+PPT录屏，格式工厂。

专家点评：用微信的形式引入，让学生先听音乐，再让学生通过新闻了解到这个乐队在全球已经风靡了50多年，以激发学生的兴趣，最后播放乐队的成员Paul McCartney在2012伦敦奥运会上演唱《Hey, Jude》的视频，使大家感受到这个乐队是多么有影响力，从而对它的歌曲感兴趣。

三、优课课例1：九年级 You're supposed to shake hands

（一）Analysis of Students（学情分析）

The students have been in the junior school for more than two and a half years. They know some of the culture of the United Kingdom. On October 20, 2015, President Xi and Ms. Peng attended the Royal dinner party in the Kingdom, so it is very good time to teach them some customs about the UK.

（二）Analysis of the Teaching Material（教材分析）

Talk about customs and what you are supposed to do.

（三）Teaching Goals（教学目标）

1. Target language

Phrases： be supposed to =be expected to =should do

2. Ability goals

（1）To develop students' ability of listening and speaking skills.

（2）To foster students' abilities of communication and their innovation.

（3）Learn how to write a composition according to the instructions.

3. Strategy goals

Task-based approach（任务型教学法），Situational approach（情境教学法），The communicative language teaching（交际教学法）.

4. Emotional goals

Learn to know more about Chinese culture and be proud of being a Chinese.

5. Teaching aid： A computer for multimedia use.（如下表所示）

Teaching procedures

Steps	Teacher's activities	Students' activities	Ways
Step 1：Organization and Warming up	1. Organization: Organize the students by greeting.	Greeting .	组织课堂，老师和学生的上课准备。
	2. Let Ss watch a video about the Royal dinner party.	Get to know something about the Royal dinner party.	通过视频引起学生的兴趣，并直接使学生进入本节课的教学。
	3. Show students the teaching aims about this lesson.	Learn about the teaching aims about this lesson.	了解本节课的教学目标。
Step 2：Presentation	1. Show a picture of Obama who looked sad. Let the students guess what's wrong with him?	Guess what's wrong with Obama.	通过猜测奥巴马在英国国宴闹笑话的视频，直接引入微课。
	2. Let students learn the micro-course.	Learn the micro-course.	通过学习微课，了解英国国宴的一些传统的文化，引入本节课的重点内容。

续表

Steps	Teacher's activities	Students' activities	Ways
Step 2: Presentation	3. Let students check the answers what should you avoid talking about during dinner conversation with other guess.	What should you avoid talking about during dinner conversation with other guess?	通过校对答案，将微课和本节课的内容联系在一起。
Step 3: Reading practice and Oral practice	1. Let students read a passage: The Royal dinner party in UK and China.	Read something about the Royal dinner party in UK and China.	根据阅读材料的内容谈论英国国宴与中国国宴的基本情况，并且为后面的作文做好铺垫。
	2. Let students talk about the difference of Royal dinner between UK and China.	Students talk about the difference of Royal dinner between UK and China.	通过口语练习，为学生的作文搭好脚手架。
Step 4: Writing	1. Let students analyze the composition.	Analyze the composition.	通过分析作文使学生知道怎样写作文。
	2. Let the students write down the phrases: be supposed to=be expected to=should do.	Write down the words and phrases they need for the composition.	熟悉单词和短语，为作文做好准备。
	3. Let the students know about the points they can get when they write down the main points.	Know about the points they can get when they write down the main points.	通过了解各个要点的分值，让学生更好地把握写作文的重点。
	4. Let the students write the composition according to what have learned today and use the good sentences in the slide.	Write the composition according to what have learned today and use the good sentences in the slide.	用本节课所学的知识写作文，并且学会运用好词好句。
	5. Let students exchange their writings and check them.	Exchange their writings and check them.	交换作文互改，让学生欣赏同学的作文，并且了解怎样修改作文。
	6. Let students write down one or two sentences from the writing and correct them.	Write down one or two sentences from the writing and correct them.	通过修改同学的作文并且修改错误的句子，让学生从学生的错误中预防错误。

续表

Steps	Teacher's activities	Students' activities	Ways
Step 4: Writing	7. Show students their correcting and check them.	Learn about the correcting.	检查学生修改错误的情况。
Step 5: Summary	Summarize what students have learned today.	Summarize the language points they have learned.	通过总结，让学生的脑海里再次呈现出这节课所学的内容，巩固所学的内容。

（四）课堂实录

Step 1：Organization and Warming up

T：Good morning, boys and girls. Today we're going to learn some customs about The Royal dinner in UK. First let's watch a video about the Royal dinner party.

Ss：Yes.

（Teacher shows the video, and lets students get to know something about the Royal dinner party.）

T：Today we are going to learn something about the Royal dinner party in the UK.

（Teacher leads to today's topic：Show the teaching aims.）

Step 2：Presentation

T：（Show a picture of Obama who looks sad.）What's wrong with him?

Ss：He looked sad.

T：Can you guess what's wrong with him?

（Ss guess the answers.）

T：The news will tell you the answers.

（Teacher lets the students watch a video of Obama made a mistake in the Royal dinner party.）

（设计意图：通过猜测，激起学生对英国国宴的一些文化习俗的兴趣，并引入微课。通过学习微课，了解英国国宴的一些传统的文化，引入本节课的重点内容。通过校对答案，将微课和本节课的内容联系在一起。）

Step 3: Reading practice and Oral practice

T: Just now, we know something Cultures of the Royal dinner party in UK, Now read a passage: Chinese Royal dinner party VS UK Royal dinner party. Then tell us what is the difference between them.

Ss: In China, men wear suits or folk costume.（中山装）

T: Yes, you have got one point.

Ss: In England, men wear cocktail dresses or folk costume.

T: What else?

Ss: Eating.

T: Yes, what the Chinese eat is quite different from the UK…

（设计意图：通过对微课的内容进行重现，让学生谈论英国国宴的一些基本情况，为后面的作文做充足的准备。）

Step 4: Writing

T: From what we have learned today, I am sure that you have got to know some customs about the Royal dinner party. Now Ms. Peng has gone back to China, she missed her trip in UK. Let's write a letter to Queen Elizabeth the Second, and invite her to come to China.

（Teacher created a situation for students to write a letter to Queen Elizabeth.）

（Teacher lets the students write the composition according to what have learned today and use the phrases "be supposed to=be expected to=should do" in the slide.）

（Teacher shows the students how to get high points in writing.）

（Teacher lets the students write down one or two sentences from the writing and correct them. Teacher shows students their correcting and check them）

（设计意图：学生根据本课话题写一封信；复习本课的新短语，为后面的作文做准备。通过分析要点，使学生了解老师的评分标准。通过修改同学的作文并且修改错误的句子，让学生从学生的错误中预防错误。检查学生修改错误的情况。）

Step 5: Summary

T: Now let's review what we have learned today. Today we have learned（1） the phrase: be supposed to= be expected to= should do. (2) Some customs about the Royal dinner party.

（设计意图：教师和学生的最后总结让学生对自己今天学习的知识进行了梳理，又一次进行了强化，加深了印象。）

四、优课课例2：Go For It 八年级上册Unit 9 Can you come to my party? （读写课）

（一）Analysis of Students（学情分析）

Students love parties, so they are interested in the topic of this unit. But as they seldom attend formal parties, they know little about the party culture, especially the party in western countries.

（二）Analysis of the Teaching Material（教材分析）

In this lesson students are going to learn about different kinds of parties and how to make an invitation, how to accept an invitation and how to turn down an invitation. In the last two period of this unit, students have learnt about the preparation and the activities of parties. In this lesson they are going to learn about the messages about parties.

（三）Teaching Goals（教学目标）

1. Target language

Can you come to my party on Saturday?

Sure, I'd love to./ Sorry, I must study for a math test.

Can he go to the party?

No, he can't. He has to help his parents.

Can they go to the movies?

No, they're not free. They might have to meet their friends.

2. Ability goals

（1）To develop students' ability of reading and writing skills.

（2）To foster students' abilities of communication and their innovation.

（3）Learn about the party culture of western countries.

3. Strategy goals

Task-based approach（任务型教学法）, Situational approach（情境教学

法), The communicative language teaching (交际教学法).

4. Emotional goals

Learn to know more about party culture and try to be polite in parties. (如下表所示)

(Teaching aid: A computer for multimedia use)

Teaching procedures

Steps	Teacher's activities	Students' activities	Ways
Step 1: Organization and Warming up	Ask students questions about party.	Answer the teacher's questions.	问答引入话题。
	Show students a mind-map about kinds of party.	Complete the mind-map and learn about the parties in China and in western countries.	思维导图呈现聚会的种类。
Step 2: Pre-reading	Ask students questions about the reading material.	Answer the questions and learn the structure of the invitation.	学习邀请函的格式。
Step 3: While-reading	Show students three reasons and the reading material.	Read the messages and match the reason with each message.	阅读配对，区分邀请函的意图。
	Show students five questions.	Read the messages again and answer the questions.	细节阅读，加深理解。
Step 4: Micro-course	Show the students a micro-course about different parties.	Watch the micro-course and take notes.	观看微课，学习聚会的不同类型。
Step 5: After-reading	Show students an invitation.	Complete the invitation with the words and phrase from the messages on page 69.	模仿写作，熟悉格式。
	Show students a writing task.	Write an invitation by themselves.	尝试写作，鼓励创新。
Step 6: Summary	Sum up what we have learn in today's lesson.	Review the structure of ab invitation.	复习巩固。
Step 7: Homework	Watch a micro-course about the party culture in western countries.		

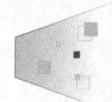

第六章
文化意识的微视频设计与实施

（四）课堂实录

Step 1： Organization and Warming up

T： Good morning, boys and girls! I know you like party, right? Did you hold a party before? Did you go to a party before? What kind of party did you go to? What did you do in the party?

（设计意图：通过自由问答，引入本节课的重点内容。）

T： What kinds of parties do you know? Finish the mind-map on your sheet.

（设计意图：通过完成思维导图，引出中国聚会的种类，特别引导学生了解西方国家常见的聚会种类。）

Step 2： Pre-reading

T： Look at the material, what kind of passage is it? What's the structure?

（设计意图：通过了解阅读材料格式，为下面的写作做铺垫。）

Step 3： While-reading

T： Read the messages quickly. Why did the people write them? Match the reason with each message.

（设计意图：通过快速阅读材料，区分三篇邀请函的写作意图，进一步熟悉格式内容。）

T： Read the messages again and answer the following questions.

Check the answers.

（设计意图：通过细节阅读，理解文章内容，学习文章语言知识点。）

Step 4： Micro-course

T： Let's watch a micro-course and learn about the introduction of different parties.

（设计意图：通过观看微课，了解国内外不同种类的聚会，学习异国文化。）

Step 5： After-reading

T： Read through the invitation and complete it with the words and phrases from the messages on page 69.

Check the answers.

（设计意图：通过补充文章邀请函，运用重点知识点。）

T： Write an invitation by yourselves according to the messages from the micro-

171

course. Try to be creative.

（设计意图：通过写邀请函，运用本课所学，发挥想象。）

Step 6: Summary

T: Now let's review what we have learned today. What kinds of party do you know?

（设计意图：教师和学生的最后总结让学生对自己今天学习的知识进行了梳理，又一次强化，加深印象。）

Step 7: Homework

Watch a micro-course about the party culture in western countries.

（设计意图：通过课后观看微课，进一步了解聚会文化。）

（五）课后反思

本节课最大的优点是在课中和课后运用了微视频作为本节课授课内容的辅助手段，让学生从不同聚会类型的介绍到国内外聚会文化，包括聚会礼仪等，全方位地学习了聚会文化，使学生受益匪浅。而聚会文化的学习也为写作提供了基础，因此本节课的活动设计环环相扣、联系紧密。

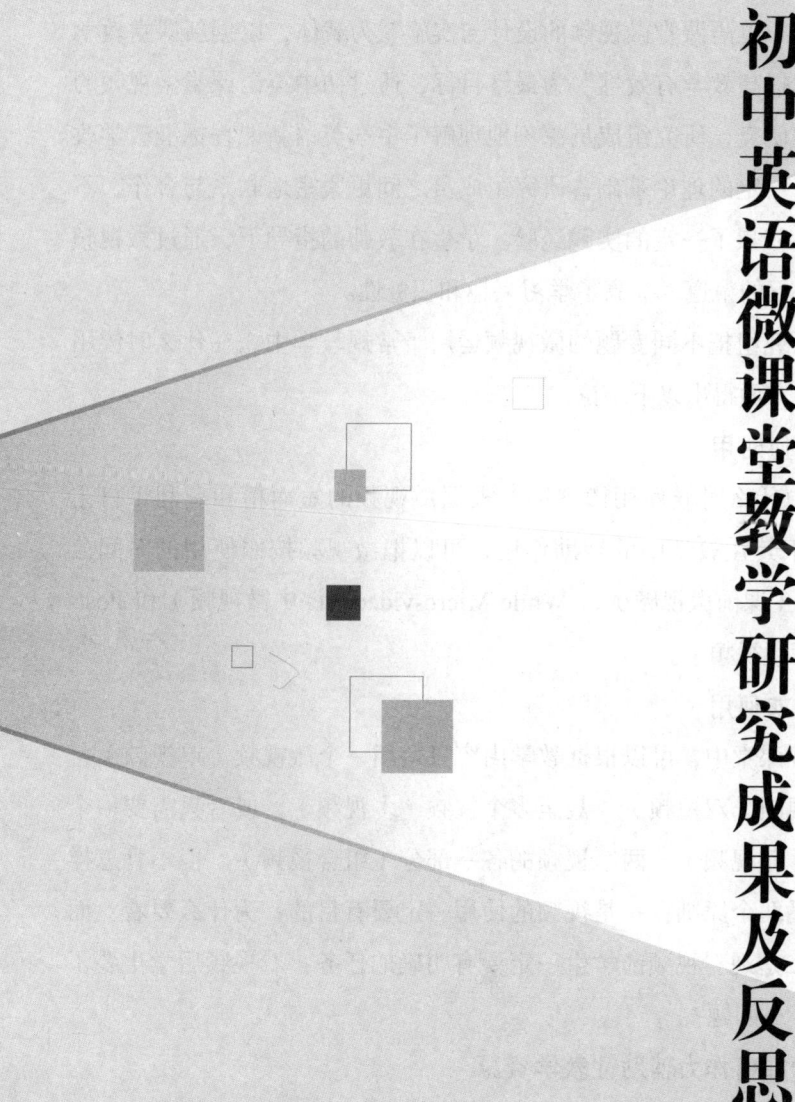

第七章 初中英语微课堂教学研究成果及反思

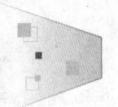
玩转英语课堂的微视频
——初中英语课堂微视频的设计与实施

经过扎实有效的研讨，我们以"理论联系实际，实践中提升教学"为指导思想，围绕课题，认真学习，探索钻研新的教学模式，按照实施方案，开展相关的研究，对"初中英语课堂微视频的设计与实施"进行了积极的探索和实践，取得了显著的成果。

一、理论性成果

本研究以"初中英语课堂微视频的设计与实施"为载体，以创新课堂教学模式为手段，以"提高教学有效性"为最终目标，通过初中英语课堂微视频的设计与实施的教学研究，研究组成员深刻地理解了中学英语新课程标准教学改革的理论，积累了一定的理论基础；研究组成员之间更紧密地联系与合作，不断优化教学模式，积累了一定的实践经验。学生在教师的指导下，通过微视频的辅助，拓展了学习的渠道，提高了学习兴趣和积极性。

经过探讨，研究组把不同专题的微视频运用于常规教学中，在什么时候用微视频和如何使用方面得出以下结论。

（一）微视频何时用

在常规课堂中什么时候使用微视频？根据微视频的短而精和有利于自主学习的特点，基于其在教学中的辅助作用，可以把微视频按照使用的时间分为Pre-Micro-video（课前微视频）、While-Micro-video（课中微视频）和Post-Micro-video（课后微视频）。

（二）微视频如何用

在同一节常规课堂中，可以根据教学内容只运用一个微视频（单视频），也可以运用两个视频（双视频），甚至多个视频（多视频），或者只需要一个微视频的一部分（截视频）、两个视频的各一部分（组合视频）。但不管怎样使用，都应该遵循两个原则：一是视频的使用一定要有目的：为什么要看？而不是盲目观看；二是观看视频前学生一定要有明确的任务：看视频后学生要了解什么？要回答什么问题？

（三）微视频如何作为辅助性教学资源

（1）作为优质教学资源，微视频对于农村薄弱学校的英语教师有帮助。

（2）作为优质教学资源，微视频对于教师结构不均衡的学校有帮助，当一位教师在课堂上怎样都无法把一个知识点讲透彻时,可以借助微视频资源。

(3)作为优质教学资源,微视频对于重复出现的知识点有作用。同一位教师教了学生三年,在讲解知识点时难免炒冷饭,借助微视频资源,会有焕然一新的作用。

二、实践性成果

1. 取得了良好的教学实践效果

实验学校是一所农村镇办初中,中考总平均分低于市平均水平。通过"初中英语课堂微视频的设计与实施"课题的研究,课题组成员以研促教,所带班级在同级同类型班级中成绩显著,课堂教学方式深受学生欢迎。

2. 直击中考语法复习,冲刺中考

从2013年中考开始,研究组成员7人,其中有4人是在九年级中考语法总复习时开始尝试使用微课。微课,就像是在平淡无味的菜里面加上了调味剂,九年级的中考语法复习紧张而乏味,加入了微课这一调味剂,不仅使学生的复习添加色彩,更使老师解脱出来。在观看微课的时候,优秀生可以自行进行复习巩固,教师则有时间去兼顾薄弱学生,进行个别辅导,教学更有针对性。因此在这样的带动下,实验学校的中考成绩有明显提高,这对于中考总平均分低于市平均水平的学校来说实属不易,2014—2016年中考英语科平均分与2011—2013年对比分析详如下图所示。

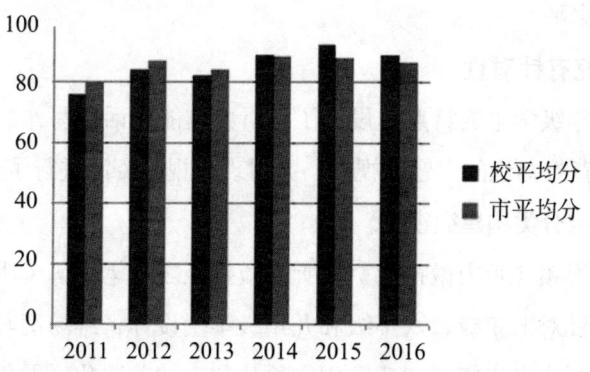

3. 促进了教师教科研能力的提升

教师参与教研，以研促教，以研促成长。在本研究的带动下，研究组有4位老师分别获评东莞市第一、第二批文科组初中英语教学能手，一位老师被聘为清溪镇第二批初中英语学科带头人，一位老师被聘为东莞市优微课评选评委，研究组成员的教学教研能力得到很大的提高。自研究开展以来，先后有30个微课作品获东莞市微课评选一等奖、二等奖、三等奖，10篇论文获东莞市优秀论文评选一等奖、二等奖、三等奖或在全国核心期刊发表，8个优课作品获东莞市优课评选一等奖、二等奖、三等奖，其中一个优课获评部级优课。

4. 发挥骨干教师的引领作用

在研究组成员的带领下，发挥骨干教师的引领作用，把好的教学经验和教研心得在英语科组里推广。在学校"青蓝工程"活动中，研究组2位老师被聘为指导老师，带领青年教师，指导效果良好。2014年4月学校组织了英语科组青年教师微课比赛，共有10位青年教师上了10节微课；2016年学校组织了英语科组青年教师微课作品比赛，共上交了13个微课作品，其中5个作品参加东莞市微课作品评选，获一等奖、三等奖。

三、研究创新表现

本研究不仅是课程改革的需要，更是解决目前我校英语教学问题的需要，同时也是智慧课堂的体现。本研究的创新点主要体现在通过把不同类型的微视频与常规课堂有机结合，激发学生课堂学习的积极性，提高课堂教学质量，提升教师的专业水平。

（一）研究有针对性

根据不同年级学生的特点，设计了以听力技能、话题写作、阅读技能、专题语法和文化背景知识的专题微视频，并对现有视频资源进行了分类构建。

1. 按知识点分类构建微视频

例如，微视频《听力微技能》《听力微技能之记笔记》《听力微技能之细节理解》分别针对七年级、八年级和九年级学生设计，难易度与学生的实际水平相符。还有写作微视频《"巧"用宾语从句，"美"化话题作文》《写作微技能之段落展开策略：举例子和归纳》《写人记叙文模板》《七下U12写作微

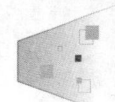

课》；阅读微视频《阅读理解之主旨大意题的解题技巧》《阅读微技能之根据配图预测文章大意》；专题语法微视频《现在完成时的"短"与"延"》《定语从句：定语从句难点突破》《现在完成时》《被动语态：被动语态难点突破》《八年级下册Unit 9 Section A 语法结构及运用》《现在进行时》《不定冠词a/an》《思维导图——语法复习的好帮手》；文化背景知识微视频《Dragon Boat Festival》《Chinese Culture》《礼貌请求》《Unit 4 The Pop Music in England》《端午节文化》《You're supposed to shake hands.》《派对礼仪》《派对文化》《中国部分习俗》《中美送礼文化之对比》等，为我们的课堂教学提供了很好的、形象生动的教学素材。

2. 按单元内容分类汇编微视频

我们把东莞市2014—2016年获奖优微课资源进行分类构建，按照单元内容对照进行整编，分成七年级上册优（微）课目录、七年级下册优（微）课目录、八年级上册优（微）课目录、八年级下册优（微）课目录、九年级优（微）课目录、中考复习优（微）课目录和中考语法优（微）课目录七个模块，优（微）课资源共享在百度云盘，供学校老师按目录检索使用。

（二）研究体现人文性

英语学科的核心素养包括语言能力、思维品质、文化品格和学习能力四个方面。文化意识重点在于理解各国文化内涵，能理解并尊重文化差异。研究组通过制作《Dragon Boat Festival》《Chinese Culture》《礼貌请求》《Unit 4 The Pop Music in England》《端午节文化》《You're supposed to shake hands.》《派对礼仪》《派对文化》《中国部分习俗》《中美送礼文化之对比》等文化背景知识专题微视频，并把微视频运用于常规课堂中，旨在通过视频让学生了解国外文化，了解各地文化差异，拓宽视野，有利于学生对这门语言的理解，也有利于培养学生优秀的文化品格。

（三）研究尝试"双师"教学

教师能力的差异也是导致教学效果不同的因素之一，特别是在教师结构不均衡的学校。在课堂上运用微视频教学，科任教师加上微视频讲解的教师同时出现在一节课的不同教学活动里面，尝试另一个模式的"双师"教学，教师花大量时间却不能讲清楚的重难点通过微视频的形式进行突破，这不但帮助了学生，还能减轻教师上课的负担。一位教师如果带同一班学生三年，相同的知识点第一次讲是新鲜，第二次讲是复习，第三次讲就是炒冷饭了，炒来炒去就烦了。重要的事情说三遍，我们日常教学中的知识点三年下来又何止是三遍可以达到效果的？如能换一种形式换一位老师，用微课的形式进行，可能就会有不一样的效果，事实也证明，优质的微课资源确实给我们的常规教学带来耳目一新的效果，也激发了学生的积极性。

（四）研究体现"智慧"课堂

研究组成员构思精巧、别出心裁的微视频设计和简洁、恰到好处的优课制作，充分体现了以教师的智慧激发学生的智慧潜能，让智慧唤醒课堂，让智慧引领教师专业成长的过程。

（五）研究成果易于分享

微视频、优课视频是研究的成果，把这些资源制作成光盘，同时保存在百度云盘，作为优质的教学资源，为其他教师进行常规教学设计提供了形象生动的实例参照，方便教师进行教学业务提升学习，提高英语教师进行教学探索的积极性。

（六）研究体现实操性

初中英语课堂微视频设计与实施调动了学生学习的积极性，提高了学生的学业成绩，提升了教师的教研能力和课堂教学水平。同时，研究组把2014—2016年东莞市获奖优微课进行分类构建，按照单元内容对照进行整编，分成七个目录模块。借助这些获奖优微课资源，凡是使用人教版《Go for it》教材的教师，都可以通过这个目录检索出每个单元的教学资源作为参考，使我们的课堂模式更加丰富多样、课堂更加精彩。

四、课题研究存在的主要问题及今后的设想

本研究虽然即将告一段落，但并未结束，围绕本研究需要我们探求的问题依然很多。例如，我们还缺乏对初中英语课堂微视频设计与实施的有效评价方案，我们应该制定一个系统的评价机制，对那些在本研究中做出突出贡献的教师们，无论是从精神上还是物质上要给予一定的奖励，以便最大限度地调动教师们参与到本课题的研究中。我们所设计的视频仍有需要改进之处，我们应

第七章
初中英语微课堂教学研究成果及反思

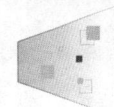

该集合大家的智慧,把视频制作好,制作精,同时探索更灵活多样的课堂教学设计。本研究结束后,全体成员将会在认真总结以往经验教训的基础上,继续努力,不断探索,坚持不懈,设计出更多系列化的微课,比如文化背景知识微视频,将其运用于课堂教学中,把常规课堂教学和学生文化品格的培养结合起来,最终把我校的英语教学工作提升到一个更高的层次!

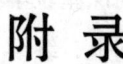

关于在英语课堂中利用微视频进行教学的问卷调查统计结果

题号	A	B	C	D	E	F	G
1	27	79	46	\	\	\	\
2	7	15	130	\	\	\	\
3	52	74	26	\	\	\	\
4	28	4	96	19	5	\	\
5	26	32	94	\	\	\	\
6	6	13	133	\	\	\	\
7	19	52	81	\	\	\	\
8	8	24	120	\	\	\	\
9	18	53	81	\	\	\	\
10	37	28	19	16	25	17	10

调查结果显示：在参加问卷调查的老师中，85%的教师从来没有在英语课堂中利用过微视频进行教学，49%的教师认为微视频的长度应该在5~10分钟比较合适，63%的教师直接使用网上下载的微视频，17%的教师认为微视频使用方便，88%的教师从未尝试过制作微视频，53%的教师认为身边的同事使用微视频对自己没有促进。

由此可见，东莞市目前英语教师对微视频的了解还比较浅，运用得也比较少，教师使用微视频的积极性也不高。而随着教育资源的丰富、教育交流的方便、学校教学设备的不断完善，在初中英语课堂上探索微视频的设计并尝试运用于课堂教学是可行的，对课堂也有一定的促进作用。

课题组成员近三年所教班级成绩与同级同类型班级对比

学期	班级	班平均分	年级平均	对比
成员A				
2014—2015上学期	七（7）、（8）	79.2	78	+1.2
2014—2015下学期	七（7）、（8）	78.1	76.6	+1.5
2015—2016上学期	八（7）、（8）	84.6	84.1	+0.5
2015—2016下学期	八（7）、（8）	85.4	84.6	+0.8
2016—2017上学期	九（7）、（8）	99.9	99.4	+0.5
成员B				
2014—2015上学期	八（7）、（8）	69.1	68.1	+1
2014—2015下学期	八（7）、（8）	66.1	62.7	+3.4
2015—2016上学期	九（8）	82.5	77.5	+5
2015—2016下学期	九（8）	93	84.2	+8.8
成员C				
2014—2015上学期	九（7）、（8）	79.7	79.1	+0.6
2014—2015下学期	九（7）、（8）	87.5	86	+1.5
2015—2016上学期	九（3）、（4）	79.7	77.5	+2.2
2015—2016下学期	九（3）、（4）	84.5	84.2	+0.3
2016—2017上学期	九（11）、（12）	79.3	81.4	-1.1
成员D				
2014—2015上学期	八（9）、（10）	83.2	82.6	+0.6
2014—2015下学期	八（9）、（10）	79.7	79.1	+0.6
2015—2016上学期	九（9）、（10）	95.1	94	+1.1
2015—2016下学期	九（9）、（10）	98.6	94.3	+4.3
2016—2017上学期	七（15）、（16）	87.9	87.3	+0.6
成员E				
2014—2015上学期	八（13）、（14）	70.9	68.1	+2.8
2014—2015下学期	八（13）、（14）	63.7	62.7	+1
2015—2016上学期	八（15）、（16）	83.6	84.6	-1
2015—2016下学期	八（15）、（16）	84.6	84.6	+0
2016—2017上学期	八（15）、（16）	81	80.9	-0.1

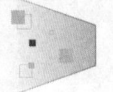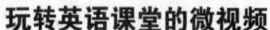

续 表

成员F				
2014—2015上学期	七（13）、（14）	73.1	73.5	-0.4
2014—2015下学期	七（13）、（14）	68.2	68.9	-0.7
2015—2016上学期	八（13）、（14）	68.8	69.7	-0.9
2015—2016下学期	八（13）、（14）	67.4	68.4	-1
2016—2017上学期	七（5）、（6）	75.4	76.6	-1.2
成员G				
2014—2015上学期	八（1）、（2）	84.9	82.6	+2.3
2014—2015下学期	八（1）、（2）	83.2	79.7	+3.5
2015—2016上学期	九（1）、（2）	100.2	95.1	+5.1
2015—2016下学期	九（1）、（2）	103.7	94.3	+9.4
2016—2017上学期	九（15）、（16）	99	99.4	-0.4

参考文献

［1］中华人民共和国教育部.基础教育课程改革纲要（试行）［M］.北京：人民教育出版社，2001.

［2］中华人民共和国教育部.义务教育英语课程标准（2011年版）［M］.北京：北京师范大学出版社，2011.

［3］Field, John. Skills and strategies: towards a new methodology for listening［J］. ELT Journal, 1998, 52（2）.

［4］卜彩丽.翻转课堂教学模式在我国高等院校应用的可行性分析［J］.软件导刊，2013.

［5］万国军.微课的设计与制作［J］.中小学电教（下），2013（5）.

［6］杨晓哲.微课，从制作到系统变革［DB/OL］.百度文库，2013.

［7］朱宇华.录屏软件在多媒体课件制作中的应用［J］.科技信息（学术研究），2006（12）.

［8］张步雯.初中英语"微课"教学分析［J］.中国教师，2014（24）.

［9］葛小花.微课视域下的初中英语课堂教学实践［J］.新课程学习（下旬）2014（10）.

［10］黄夏芹.基于微课理论的初中英语课堂教学［J］.中学生英语（外语教学与研究），2014（8）.

［11］张金磊.翻转课堂教学模式研究［J］.远程教育杂志，2012.

［12］张志宏.微课，一种新型的学习资源［J］.中国教育技术装备，2013.

［13］倪扬英.一堂优质课对阅读文本解读的几点启示［J］.中小英语教学与研究，2015.

［14］马琳玉.整合教学资源开展中职英语阅读教学的案例研究［J］.中小学英语教学与研究，2015（2）.

［15］黄少华，杨亚军.高考阅读理解主旨大意题的易错原因探析［J］.新东方英语（中学生），2014（11）.

［16］韩秀荣.英文电影在初中英语教学中的应用研究［D］.西安：陕西师范大学，2012.

［17］黄光雄，蔡清田.核心素养课程发展与设计新论［M］.上海：华东师范大学出版社，2017.

［18］赵婷.微视频在八年级英语教学中的实践研究［D］，银川：宁夏大学，2014.

［19］程晓堂，郑敏.英语学习策略［M］.北京：外语教学与研究出版社，2002.

［20］张一春.微课建设研究与思考［J］.中国教育网络，2013（10）.

［21］丁庆娟.九年级英语复习课有效教学探究——从一次市级公开课"话题式"复习谈起［J］.中学英语（初中教师版），2011.

［22］徐嫦华.以话题为模块开展九年级英语词汇总复习——以food话题为例［J］.教学月刊（中学版），2011.

［23］姚仁环.九年级英语单元话题模块重组的教学实践与反思［J］.中小学英语教学与研究，2010.

［24］戴军熔.基于话题的立体式语言教学的设计与实施［J］.中小学外语教学（中学篇），2010.

［25］毛克民.九年级英语话题式复习教学的实践与思考［J］.英语教师，2013.

［26］费晨.A Father and a Son阅读课教学设计［J］.中小学外语教学（中学篇），2017（3）.

［27］课程教材研究所.义务教育教科书教师教学用书（八年级下册）［M］.北京：人民教育出版社，2014.

［28］中华人民共和国教育部.普通高中英语课程标准（2017年版）［M］.北京：人民教育出版社，2017.

［29］李莎.初中英语教师跨文化意识发展模型研究［D］.重庆：西南大学，2010.